Value Me

VALUE ME

SHELAGH BROWN WITH
PHIL LAWSON JOHNSTON

 The Bible Reading Fellowship

Published by
The Bible Reading Fellowship
Peter's Way, Sandy Lane West
Oxford OX4 5HG
ISBN 0 7459 2990 7
Albatross Books Pty Ltd
PO Box 320, Sutherland
NSW 2232, Australia
ISBN 0 7324 0919 5

First edition 1995
10 9 8 7 6 5 4 3 2 1 0

Acknowledgments
Unless otherwise stated, scripture is taken from The Holy Bible,
New International Version copyright © 1973, 1978, 1984 by
International Bible Society. Used by permission.

The Good News Bible (GNB) published by The Bible Societies/
HarperCollins Publishers Ltd, UK © American Bible Society
1966, 1971, 1976, 1992.

Revised English Bible (REB) © 1989 by permission of Oxford
and Cambridge University Presses.

Revised Standard Version of the Bible (RSV), copyright © 1946,
1952, 1971 by the Division of Christian Education of the National
Council of the Churches of Christ in the USA.

New Revised Standard Version of the Bible (NRSV), copyright ©
1989 by the Division of Christian Education of the National
Council of the Churches of Christ in the USA.

A catalogue record for this book is available
from the British Library

Printed and bound in Great Britain
by Cox and Wyman Ltd, Reading

*To protect the anonymity of contributors, several of the names and
details have been changed.*

CONTENTS

INTRODUCTION:
IMMORTAL DIAMOND

You might be someone who has a deep sense of your own worth and value—and who knows that every human being is also of great worth. You might also have a deep awareness of God's enormous love for you—and for the whole world and every person in it.

There are some rare people like that, and perhaps you are one of them. Such people are a delight to meet, because they can make us aware of our own worth. But most of us aren't very aware of it. Most of us have to discover our own value—and sometimes that can take us half a lifetime.

The beautiful and brilliant diamond on the cover of *Value Me* is there because the designer, Gerald Rogers, wanted a picture that made an unmistakable statement about value—and De Beers found just the right photograph for us.

'Diamonds are the ultimate treasure,' wrote Graham Richard in *Focus on Diamonds*—and in a material sense they are. But not in a spiritual sense. Human beings are the ultimate treasure—and each one of us is worth more than the whole world. We would never dare to believe that if Jesus hadn't said it—and some of us daren't believe it anyway.

One night a man was speaking at a Christian convention in the USA. After the meeting had ended he found himself under great sexual temptation, so he left the hall and walked out into the streets—looking for a prostitute. When he found one he asked her what her price was. But when she told him he said to her, 'It's not enough.' As he turned away from his own temptation he told her that she was worth more than the whole world—and that because he loved her so much Jesus Christ had died for her. 'Yes, I know that,' said the woman, 'I knew him once.' Then she turned away and went back to her work. The man, repentant now, and turning back to God, went back alone to his hotel room.

Phil Lawson Johnston and I heard that story in a talk on self-worth at a Spring Harvest holiday week. We were both on the team: Phil was leading the music and I was leading meditative Bible readings. We have always remembered the story, and all the time both of us are meeting people who have very little self-worth, and very little awareness of their own value.

So we decided to write a book and also produce a cassette of songs and Bible readings for all those people. People who would love to know that they really are valuable and precious—and who would love to be loved. *Value Me* identifies some of the conditions and circumstances which cause so many of us to suffer from a sense of worthlessness and a lack of self-worth. It tells how people's lives begin to change as they realize and accept where their true value lies—and at the end of the book we show ways in those who want to can start to discover this for themselves, working either on their own or in a small group.

We have called that section *Working with God*, because that is what we shall be doing. The Apostle Paul told the Christians in Philippi (and it applies just as much to us) to 'work out your salvation with fear and trembling, for it is God who works in you to will and to act according to his good purpose' (Philippians 2:12–13). Our salvation is our wholeness and our healing, part of the new life that we are given in Christ.

But the new life starts like a tiny seed—like the start of a baby. All its wonderful possibilities and its awesome potential are within it, but the child has to grow—and the God who created every child out of his love will show us the way to grow, and to be recreated and made whole. In *The Sunday Times Magazine* Archbishop Desmond Tutu told of the way he begins his day—praying like a tiny child:

> Usually I get up at 4 a.m. It's quiet and peaceful at that time, which I need to collect myself. It's a time when I try to engage with God. It's meditation. I try to centre myself on God so that He influences the rest of the day...
>
> During part of this time I kneel and then I crouch almost like a foetus. There is something about becoming a baby in the presence of God, being embraced, being

7

dandled and being made to know that you are special
and precious and loved.

It's not because I can rush into Lesotho and out again,
and appear on television; it's not because I'm an
archbishop that gives me worth: worth comes as a gift
from God, free of charge. I have gradually come to
accept this. But constantly I have to be reminded,
because I love to be loved so much.

In *Working with God* there is a reflection based on Desmond
Tutu's way of praying. There is also a reflection on a diamond—
because as we reflect on the nature and qualities of a diamond we
can discover even more about our own nature. Each diamond is
found as a rough diamond—and it takes an expert to know its value.
Each diamond is unique—because diamonds are made of crystals,
and each crystal in the whole world is different. A diamond can
reflect the light—and the whole skill of the diamond cutter is to cut it
in such a way that the diamond sparkles and shines with the greatest
possible brilliance. We can shine with the glory of God, and we can
know a freedom that we never knew before: 'Now the Lord is the
Spirit, and where the Spirit of the Lord is, there is freedom. And we,
who ... all reflect the Lord's glory, are being transformed into his
likeness with ever-increasing glory, which comes from the Lord,
who is the Spirit' (2 Corinthians 3:17–18).

Each one of us is of far greater value than all the diamonds in the
world—and God wants us to know how great our value is and how
much we are worth. So Phil has written a special song with the title
'Value me'. It starts with a request to God: 'Tell me I'm valued, tell me
I'm loved,' and it ends with the delighted discovery that 'You value
me!' In between there is questioning and longing, and words that
point us to the healing power of God in Christ.

The book takes us on the same journey as the song. Starting with
the longing—and ending with the finding. You will meet other
people on the journey—people who are on their own journey, who
have talked to us, and allowed us to share their stories. They are
people with very different stories to tell. People who have never had

any sense of value. People who feel worthless. People with broken hearts. People who hurt because of what they have lost: their health, their husband, their job or their home. A singer who lost her voice when her husband left her. A Member of Parliament who lost his career. A man who slept on the streets because he was homeless. A former prostitute. Women who suffered abuse as children. A student who had anorexia.

All these people are discovering their true worth—and their enormous value and preciousness to God. God loves each one of us because he created us—and it is because he loves us that Christ died for us.

As well as people's stories you will find here the great Christian truths and Bible passages about the love of Christ and his power to redeem and restore every person who comes to him. But the healing process hardly ever happens overnight. Like a newly planted seed of hope, it takes time to grow up into its full glory. And, as it grows, the person is able to say to God with ever-inceasing confidence and delight, 'You value me!'

The poet-priest Gerard Manley Hopkins wrote about the glory of the resurrection morning, and the transformation of being in Christ and being what Christ is. The change will be complete then. But the transformation starts now—because a Christian is in Christ now.

> In a flash, at a trumpet crash,
> I am all at once what Christ is, since he was what I am, and
> This Jack, joke, poor potsherd, patch, matchwood,
>   immortal diamond,
>   Is immortal diamond.

I WILL CHANGE YOUR NAME

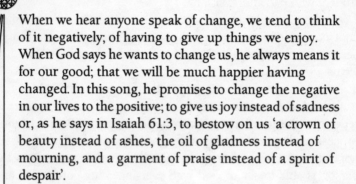

When we hear anyone speak of change, we tend to think of it negatively; of having to give up things we enjoy. When God says he wants to change us, he always means it for our good; that we will be much happier having changed. In this song, he promises to change the negative in our lives to the positive; to give us joy instead of sadness or, as he says in Isaiah 61:3, to bestow on us 'a crown of beauty instead of ashes, the oil of gladness instead of mourning, and a garment of praise instead of a spirit of despair'.

I will change your name
You shall no longer be called
Wounded, outcast,
Lonely or afraid.

I will change your name
Your new name shall be
Confidence, joyfulness,
Overcoming one,
Faithfulness, friend of God,
One who seeks My face.

D.J. Butler © Mercy Publishing/Thankyou Music 1987

In *The Muppet Movie* Kermit the Frog is sitting on a big green leaf on a pond playing his guitar and singing a song. It's a song about change, and about a voice that he can hear calling him to change—into the person that he wants to be and that he knows he is supposed to be.

Have you been down the street
And have you heard voices?
I've heard them calling my name.
Is this the sweet sound
That calls the young sailor?
The voice might be one and the same.
I've heard it too many times to ignore it,
It's something that I'm s'posed to be.
Some day we'll find it, the rainbow connection,
The lovers, the dreamers and me.

Paul Williams/Kenny Ascher © ATV Music Limited 1979

The sweet sound that the sailors heard in Greek mythology was the voice of the sirens luring them to destruction. But there is another voice that calls to us—the voice of the Creator God.

Kermit the Frog can be a symbol for all of us. Not frogs, but human beings—longing for a love that will never fail us, and longing for our dreams to come true. Listening to voices that tell us different things—and often the voices that we have heard in the past have been horribly destructive.

Little children often have to listen to a parent saying appallingly destructive words to them—and verbal abuse can do just as much damage as physical abuse. Mary's father would scream abuse at her. 'You can't do anything. You're useless. You're hopeless. Get out of my sight—you make me sick.' Mary believed what her father said about her, so she felt useless and she felt worthless.

But then one day Mary heard another voice speaking to her, and she believed what it said. The voice of God was telling her that he loved her, and the voice of Jesus was calling her to himself. Promising to satisfy the deep thirst inside her and to give her eternal life. That is what Jesus promised to a Samaritan woman he talked to sitting by a well—a woman who had had five husbands and who was currently living with a man she wasn't married to: 'All those who drink this water will be thirsty again, but whoever drinks the water that I will give him will never be thirsty again. The water that I will give him will become in him a spring which will provide him with life-giving water and give him eternal life' (John 4:14, GNB). That Samaritan woman's life started to change—and so did Mary's life.

I recently saw a television programme about plastic surgery. It wasn't about surgery on people whose faces or bodies were damaged or scarred, but on people who didn't like their faces or their bodies and wanted them to be changed. I was fascinated and horrified at the same time. I couldn't stop watching, but sometimes I closed my eyes so that I couldn't see the surgeon's knife cutting through the skin and into the flesh. Those people must have had a deep desire to change.

But there is a different sort of change, and a different sort of surgeon. T.S. Eliot likened God to a surgeon:

> The wounded surgeon plies the steel
> That questions the distempered part;
> Beneath the bleeding hands we feel
> The sharp compassion of the healer's art

T.S. Eliot, 'East Coker', in Four Quartets, © 1940, Faber & Faber Ltd

But we aren't at all sure that we want to have surgery. Most of us fear it. Most of us don't turn to the surgeon until we have to, and when our condition is so serious that there doesn't seem to be any alternative. We might have been able to have preventive treatment at an earlier stage, but a lot of us put that off as well.

When the top religious men criticized Jesus for the company he kept, he answered them by talking about the people who needed him and whom he had come to heal:

> While Jesus was having dinner at Matthew's house, many tax collectors and 'sinners' came and ate with him and his disciples. When the Pharisees saw this, they asked his disciples, 'Why does your teacher eat with tax collectors and "sinners"?' On hearing this, Jesus said, 'It is not the healthy who need a doctor, but the sick. But go and learn what this means: "I desire mercy, not sacrifice." For I have not come to call the righteous, but sinners.'

Matthew 9:10–13

Jesus, who is God in human form, is the divine physician and the wounded surgeon. Many of us are wounded too, not by what we have done to ourselves, but by what other people have done to us. 'He was despised and rejected by men,' wrote Isaiah, pointing down the years to the coming of Christ, 'a man of sorrows, and familiar with suffering' (Isaiah 53:3).

A tragically large number of people were despised and rejected when they were children. Some of them suffered physical abuse and some of them, like Mary, suffered verbal abuse. In spite of all the hideous things he said to her, Mary still loved her father, and she was terrified of being rejected by him. But he rejected her all through her childhood and adulthood, right up until the day he died.

Now Mary is disovering her own value. Discovering that she isn't useless and that she isn't hopeless. Slowly, through her experience of the love of God, she is being healed, and you can read the whole of her story in chapter 5. That same experience of inner healing, and a growing awareness of their worth and value, is common to all the people who tell their stories in *Value Me*. They have heard the voice of Jesus calling to them, and they have put themselves into the wounded hands of God. So they are being changed—into a new person with a new name.

In the Bible, a person's name stands for the person's character. Right back in the book of Genesis, God calls Abram to be the father of the people of God. But Abram's wife Sarai is barren, and although they long for a child they have never been able to have one. Then, when Abram is ninety-nine and Sarai is ninety, God makes what seems an impossible promise to Abram. 'You will be the father of many nations. No longer will you be called Abram [which means 'exalted father']; your name will be Abraham [which means 'father of many'], for I have made you a father of many nations' (Genesis 17:4).

If we feel that our own condition is hopeless, and that things can never get better, then the story of Abraham can be a light in our darkness. As we read it and reflect on it we might start to dare to hope, just as Abraham did. The Apostle Paul wrote about him to the Christians in Rome:

He is the father of us all. As it is written: 'I have made you a father of many nations.' He is our father in the sight of God, in whom he believed—the God who gives life to the dead and calls things that are not as though they were. Against all hope, Abraham in hope believed and so became the father of many nations, just as it had been said of him, 'So shall your offspring be.' Without weakening in his faith, he faced the fact that his body was as good as dead—since he was about a hundred years old—and that Sarah's womb was also dead. Yet he did not waver through unbelief regarding the promise of God, but was strengthened in his faith and gave glory to God, being fully persuaded that God had power to do what he had promised.

Romans 4:16–21

It may be that we have a very low sense of value or self-worth. Or perhaps things are so bad that we don't have any at all. Our value and our self-worth are non-existent. Then we can remind ourselves that our God 'gives life to the dead and calls things that are not as though they were.' The God who created the worlds and the galaxies by speaking his word in the darkness can create a new name and a new nature for each one of us. What we have to do is to dare to put ourselves into the wounded hands of the divine surgeon—and to allow him to work in us, and to remake us.

That is what the song 'I will change your name' is all about. Christ makes a promise to us: 'You shall no longer be called wounded, outcast, lonely or afraid... your new name shall be confidence, joyfulness, overcoming one, faithfulness, friend of God, one who seeks My face.'

God wants to transform us, and he wants us to know how much he loves us and delights in us. One of the ways to realize that is to listen to his voice through the words that he speaks in the New Testament and in the Old. Hundreds of years before the birth of Jesus, Isaiah was telling what wonderful things God can do for us:

For Zion's sake I will not keep silent,
for Jerusalem's sake I will not remain quiet,
till her righteousness shines out like the dawn,
her salvation like a blazing torch.
The nations will see your righteousness,
and all kings your glory;
you will be called by a new name
that the mouth of the Lord will bestow.
You will be a crown of splendour in the Lord's hand,
a royal diadem in the hand of your God.
No longer will they call you Deserted,
or name your land Desolate.
But you will be called Hephzibah, and your land Beulah;
for the Lord will take delight in you,
and your land will be married.
As a young man marries a maiden,
so will your sons marry you;
as a bridegroom rejoices over his bride,
so will your God rejoice over you.

Isaiah 62:1–5

It was thousands of years ago that God changed Abram's name and gave him the new name of Abraham. But God doesn't change, and he is still doing the same things now as he did then. Charles Smith's story and Martin's story are very different—but both of them tell about the unchanging power of the living God to change our name.

Charles Smith's story

Charles Smith used to be a Member of Parliament. He wanted to be in politics more than anything in the whole world, but something happened to him which cut his career short in mid-stream. There was a major Inland Revenue investigation into the company that he worked for. As the salesman Charles didn't have anything to do with the company's tax affairs. He was sure they were totally honourable, but he was included in the investigations.

They went on for four years, and Charles told his constituents that if things weren't cleared up by the next election he would stand down. They weren't cleared up, so he did stand down—and just two weeks after the election the company was cleared and so was Charles.

'So I had the enormous pain of knowing that I had thrown my entire career away for nothing,' he said. 'The agony of it was unendurable. For two years I couldn't talk about it. I was thirty-eight years old and my career had completely ended. It was what I had wanted to do more than anything else in the world.'

Charles went through a sort of dry nervous breakdown. He was very bitter and very angry. He thought about committing suicide and he thought about emigrating. 'I contemplated practically everything there was,' he said, 'and that was the negative side of my life. But the positive side was that I had a wife and children who loved me, and they managed to put up with me. I also had two friends who did the same. When something like that happens you can't find a way of avoiding the pain so you pretend that everything's all right. Outwardly prosperous, inwardly bankrupt. That's probably the best way to describe it.'

But one day Charles read a book—*Born Again*, by Chuck Colson. 'Anthony Cordle gave it to me,' he said, 'and it was a wonderful book. After I had read it I came to the Lord at a prayer breakfast in Washington in 1987.'

Charles didn't experience any blinding lights or revelation in his life, and although he had started to follow Jesus it was a very slow process. 'I resisted enormously,' he said. 'One always does, because one's such a bloody fool!'

One day he told his wife and children that he wanted to go to a Christian house party and he wanted them to come with him. They weren't at all enthusiastic, because they thought it would be very boring. But he persuaded them. The speaker at the house party was the Reverend John Collins—and through what he said the whole of Charles' family became Christians.

'They weren't rat-baggy people to start with,' said Charles, 'but I have found it astonishingly humbling to see how the Holy Spirit has worked through my wife and my children. God has changed their lives, and the way in which the fruits of their love have manifested themselves has been a wonder to see.

'So that's a wonderful story', said Charles, 'But it's also the story of folly and great misfortune. Because although I wasn't guilty of what the Revenue thought I was guilty of, I was guilty of lots of other things, which nobody knew about.'

Charles began to understand far more about himself. 'How one could be crushed by the world, and how one had to redeem it. Through the prayer and the love of my friends I came through it all,' he said, 'and in a way I triumphed—through the workings of Christ. What happened made me enormously sympathetic to other people. It also made me intensely self-aware in a way that I hadn't been before. I still do silly things and make mistakes. But now I can see—and before I was blind.'

Charles loves Gerard Hughes' books, and through reading them he has learned how to use his own weakness as the bridge to God. 'You can be so aware of your sin,' he said, 'that you feel you are blocked from God and that you can't come close to him. But Gerard Hughes suggests using one's weaknesses and inabilities as a method of connecting to God. Talking to God. Saying things like, "Here I am! I'm horrible and silly…"—whatever it is you're feeling about yourself. But coming to him, and talking to him absolutely honestly about the way you are. It's a sort of conversation piece—like that lovely poem by George Herbert.'

Love bade me welcome, yet my soul drew back,
    Guilty of dust and sin.
But quick-ey'd Love, observing me grow slack
    From my first entrance in,
Drew nearer to me, sweetly questioning
    If I lack'd any thing.

'A guest', I answer'd, 'worthy to be here.'
    Love said, 'You shall be he.'

'I the unkind, ungrateful? Ah my dear,
I cannot look on thee.'
Love took my hand, and smiling did reply,
'Who made the eyes but I?'

'Truth, Lord, but I have marr'd them; let my shame
Go where it doth deserve.'
'And know you not', says Love, 'who bore the blame?'
'My dear, then I will serve.'
'You must sit down', says Love, 'and taste my meat.'
So I did sit and eat.

'The trouble with the English,' said Charles, 'is that we think church is for virtuous people and wonderful people and sinless people. But the gorgeous thing is that God loves the foolish, the drunkards, the criminals and the murderers every bit as much as he loves the virtuous and the saintly. So many people's lives are simply diversions to stop them thinking about the eternal truths of God, and about pain and suffering and death.'

Charles Smith's own pain and suffering when his career came to an end were what finally drove him into the arms of God. Now his life has totally changed, and he does a different job.

For several years he has been running an organization which works for the men and women who were 'Names' in Lloyd's and who have suffered tremendous financial losses. Charles works with another Christian. 'We try to get better terms for the people who have suffered, and who have been traduced,' said Charles, 'and even more importantly we try and help them to come to terms with their losses and the difficulties in their lives.'

Charles links up with a nationwide organization called 'Work of Christians', and they try to put people who are in a state of trauma in touch with people who care. 'In our very materialistic society,' Charles said, 'people often see themselves as a sum of their wealth and their spending power, and when that all goes and they have lost everything they often suffer an identity crisis and feel that they are non-people.

'Our job is to try to help them to come to terms with all the things that have happened—and to realize that they are much-loved by God. We stretch out a hand of friendship to them, and we counsel them. They are in a tremendous amount of pain, and because of what happened to me I know something of what it's like for them.

'When I lost my parliamentary seat it caused me enormous trauma and enormous sadness. But that really changed my life. It made me come to terms with the Lord and it made me understand the redeeming power of Christ at first hand. It made me realize that you only learn through suffering—and that without pain you cannot learn. When you are suffering enormous pain you only have two alternatives. Either you try and anaesthetize it—with alcohol or drugs or activity or suicide. Or else you accept the pain and live through it.

'Then you start to realize that there is an inevitable connection between pain and living a full life, and there is no way that you can avoid it. Somehow you have to redeem the pain and redeem the problem.

'When you think you have let your family down you can know that they forgive you and you can know that God forgives you. But it's enormously hard to forgive yourself. Yet it is very important that you should forgive yourself—so you have to learn how to do it.'

Charles knows that his ministry is to share some of his own experience with people who are going through the same sort of suffering.

'All the people I meet now,' he said, 'are completely crushed by their adversity. A lot of them can't face the fact that to some extent they are responsible for what has happened, so they try to pretend that other people are responsible. And to some degree that is true. But ultimately people are always responsible for themselves, and my job is to try to help them to come to terms with that.'

Charles tries to help them to accept the pain—and to learn from it and to grow through it. If a person can learn to do that then the process of healing has started.

Charles is also concerned that there should be healing for the whole family, because if someone has lost their money then the whole family is affected by it. 'Wives often do forgive their husbands,' he said, 'but not always. When they have lost their homes and almost everything else then sometimes the wife will blame the husband and get very vengeful.

'Our society puts enormous pressure on you if you are a husband. You need to perform. To get out there and do things. Then when things go wrong it is terribly easy for men to think they are a total failure. That is why they often have such a terrible identity crisis if they lose their money and their job.'

'Do you mean,' I said to Charles, 'that their value consists of being a provider and a good provider?' 'Yes,' he said. 'That is the sum of their value and their status in society. You can see it all around us—the way in which we worship image and money and power. But when that's all stripped away we find that it was nothing. Like grass, it says in the Bible: "All men are like grass, and all their glory is like the flowers of the field; the grass withers and the flowers fall, but the word of the Lord stands for ever" (1 Peter 1:24–25).

'At one level we aren't of any value at all,' said Charles. 'In worldly terms we are all swept away. We dance about. We are like the grass. We are blown away. But on another level we are the most priceless things in the world—priceless beyond measure, because we are loved by Christ.'

Paddy's story

Every human being in the whole world is loved by Christ. It has nothing to do with our behaviour, our background, our race or our colour. Paddy's background is very different from Charles'. He has been to prison and he has lived on the streets.

People used to call him Paddy because of his violent temper. But he was christened Martin in the Catholic Church, and at his confirmation the name of Patrick was given to him as well. While he was still at school he started to sniff glue and then went on to drugs. 'I wasn't getting on very well at school,' he said, 'and I was very bullied. But then I'd get zonked and it would give me confidence—so that I wasn't scared any more.'

Paddy's parents weren't ideal. 'My stepmum never showed me any love,' he said. 'So long as I didn't cause too much trouble she wasn't interested. Nobody gave a damn about me. And I didn't give a damn about my parents or my family or anyone.'

He was put into care, but he was stealing to support his drug habit. He was sent to a detention centre—a young person's prison. When he got out he went back to the gang he had grown up with.

'They were the family that I never had,' Paddy said. 'If you were in the gang you were one of them, and they'd protect you. If a stranger from another gang hurts you then your gang has to hurt each and every one of them. I couldn't fight physically, but I used to carry knives about with me. And I'd carry guns. I've never actually shot anyone, but I've come quite close to it a few times.'

But the gang had their own laws. 'There would be no going up to old ladies and mugging them,' Paddy said. 'That was against our religion. It was taboo. You just didn't do it. And you didn't hurt a child.'

If anyone did hurt a child or mug an old lady the gang would punish them. 'They would be very seriously hurt,' said Paddy, 'and if they managed to get away from us and went to prison one of us would be sure to know somebody in that prison so they would cop it in there.'

Paddy never liked violence, but he still got involved in it. In one incident they were after someone who had done the dirty on their gang, and someone else knew who it was but wouldn't tell them his name. So the gang kicked him—and then cut his back up with a carving knife. But he still wouldn't talk, so they poured bleach into the cuts. Finally they poured in industrial cleaner and then he cracked—and told them the name they wanted to know.

'Did that make you feel big and strong?' I asked Paddy, and he nodded and grinned. 'Yes, very. And I've got a smile saying this— but I am very ashamed of what I used to do. I have never ever liked violence. Considering what I've just said that might be very hard to believe, but I got into violence because of the situation I was brought up in. If you weren't good at something within that circle then you were nothing—and I found I was very good at being aggressive.

'I'm not proud of what I did then, and I'm not aggressive any more. But the way I was brought up was, "Well, if you're good at anything then prove that you're good at it." Then you're respected.'

There was a fierce gang loyalty. 'They have gone to jail for me,' said Paddy, 'and I had gone to jail for them. I'd done over eight years in prison for different crimes—for violence, for burglaries and for street robberies.'

Then Paddy met Kim, and they had a child. 'I thought that would change me,' Paddy said, 'and I wanted it to change me. But I was still going about with the same people, and Kim didn't like it. She couldn't understand that these people were my family.'

Kim came from a different background from Paddy. 'She had gone to boarding school,' he said. 'She was a good, well-brought-up young lady, and what she saw in me I'll never know. But she could never understand that I couldn't let go of my friends and my family, so we split up. It was all my fault. I thought I couldn't live without them, but it turns out now that I can.'

After they split up Paddy went on a very bad alcoholic binge that lasted for nearly three years. Even his gang started to tell him that things were getting serious. 'I was stinking,' he said, 'and my jeans had about two inches of dirt on them.' He was sleeping rough because he was banned from every night shelter in the town that looked after the homeless.

Paddy was drinking two and a half bottles of vodka a day plus cans of lager. He was admitted to hospital, but one day he discharged himself. 'I went straight for the vodka', he said, 'and I was drinking it with a bloke called Bruno on the steps of the bus station. Then two girls and a bloke came up to us and offered us some soup and sandwiches.

'My friend Bruno is a diabetic, and he eats like a horse. So he had a sandwich. But I was saying to him, "No! What are you doing? They're the last people I want to get involved with. No way."'

Paddy didn't want to get involved because they had told him they were Christians. 'They asked me if I wanted some food,' he said, 'But I said "No! I'm quite happy with my bottle, thank you. Leave me alone." Then they started talking to Bruno, and we all started talking.

"I've got respect for what you're doing," I said to them, "and I respect you. But don't talk to me about this Christian stuff because I don't want to know."'

They didn't talk to him—but they got him to promise to come to church on the next Sunday. The service was held in a hall, not a church, and on the Sunday morning Paddy went to it. 'I just sat there smelling to high heaven,' he said, 'and Bruno and another lad came. Then the band started playing, and I thought, "Yes, this is really good." Especially the songs. As far as I was concerned they were better than the sermon. They were saying everything that needed to be said.'

Paddy had been brought up a Catholic and gone to Catholic schools, so he was used to a far more traditional service. This was totally different. 'Hang on!' he thought, 'This isn't religion! This is just a gig.'

But he was enjoying it, so when the two girls asked him to a meeting during the week he agreed to go. At that moment the flute player came up, and Paddy said to him, 'I've got to tell you—I really like the way you play that thing. You remind me of Pink Floyd. You're so laid back, and you just go into it.'

The flute player was Mike, who plays the flute on the *Value Me* tape. 'He's amazing,' said Paddy. 'He plays brilliantly—and he really knocked me back.'

Every week for two months Paddy kept coming back to the service. The music and the words were making sense to him and getting through to him. People were offering to pray with him, but to begin with he wouldn't let them. However, he couldn't stop them praying for him, and that is what they were doing.

One reason why Paddy kept coming back to the service was that he could have a decent conversation there. 'It gets boring,' he said, 'if all you talk about for seven days a week is, "Where are we getting the money for a bottle? Who are we going to mug? Who are we going to beat the crap out of?"

'I had listened to that for fifty-two weeks a year for nearly ten years. Then all of a sudden I was put in a situation where I could spend one day a week talking to people who didn't bring up violence or alcohol or sex. It didn't matter what I looked like. I could sit down and have a decent conversation. So I kept on going.'

Sometimes people would talk to Paddy about what it said in the Bible. 'They would quote me bits', he said, 'and I would tell them I knew it. "How do you know it?" they'd ask me. So one day I told them. I had read it when I was doing five months' solitary confinement in prison!

'By this time I knew Phil and I knew the band. I knew everyone in there. I was still sleeping on the streets. I was still smelly. But people would come up and say, "It's nice to see you" and give me cuddles. And I'd think, "How can you cuddle me? I'm stinking!"'

Paddy was still drinking, but he wouldn't drink on a Sunday. 'I had respect for the people in the service,' he said. 'And I saw them all being naturally happy. They didn't need drugs. They didn't need to get high. What I saw was defying all the ways I got high—from drugs and alcohol.

'One day I said, "There's something here." I saw students who were poorer than me. I could guarantee money every day. They couldn't. But they were literally jumping around with joy. And something just went inside me. I thought, "If this Jesus is there I want a piece of this..." So I went up and said, "If anyone needs prayer it's me!" Little did I know that everybody had been praying for me—all over Oxfordshire! I was shaking like a leaf, but when they prayed for me my shakes stopped.'

The shakes came back again, and Paddy went into the town and got a drink again. But he came back the following Sunday and asked them to pray for him again. 'I walked up to them,' he said, 'and I told them I'm still drinking. I know it's there, but I don't know what it is. Just help me." They prayed for me, and the shakes stopped completely.

'Then I heard someone say to me, "Do you believe that Jesus died on the cross for your sins." And I said "Yes." At that moment I did believe—and I still do.'

After that Paddy didn't drink for six months. Then he had a lapse—and he still has lapses. 'But before I committed myself to the Lord,' he said, 'I wasn't happy when I went on the dry. Now when I go on the dry I am happy—and I can't explain it.

But now, this is what the Lord says—he who created you, O Jacob, He who formed you, O Israel: 'Fear not, for I have redeemed you; I have summoned you by name; you are mine. When you pass through the waters, I will be with you; and when you pass through the rivers, they will not sweep over you. When you walk through the fire, you will not be burned; the flames will not set you ablaze. For I am the Lord, your God, the Holy One of Israel, your Saviour; I give Egypt for your ransom, Cush and Seba in your stead. Since you are precious and honoured in my sight, and because I love you.

Isaiah 43:1–4

He who has an ear, let him hear what the Spirit says to the churches. To him who overcomes, I will give some of the hidden manna. I will also give him a white stone with a new name written on it, known only to him who receives it.

Revelation 2:17

'I know that the Lord is looking after me, because if he wasn't I'd have been dead a long time ago. I've OD'd countless times. I've been tortured with a Stanley knife. I've been shot in the bottom of the leg. And if I wasn't dead I'd be doing life imprisonment.'

Paddy still sees his old gang, but if they are going off to fight or to brawl they won't tell him. 'That's because they respect my point of view,' Paddy said. 'I think that really each and every one of them wants to come in contact with the Lord, because they want the natural happiness that they would have if they did. But none of them have got the guts to make the choice. That's not putting me on a pedestal, because I don't think I had much choice in the matter. It just dawned on me—and then it happened.'

It is only recently that Paddy has started to get in touch with his emotions. 'Before I committed my life to the Lord I was empty,' he said. 'I felt physical pain, but it didn't bother me. The pain would go on for a certain length of time, but then it was gone. When I was tortured I had seventeen stitches in my face, four in my arm and seven on my head. But when they had finished torturing me I just walked away.

'I didn't hate them. I couldn't. I couldn't feel any emotions. It was just that they had got me before I got them—and if I'd known they were trying to get me then I'd have beaten them to it. That was the life I lived. It was clear cut. They do you—you do them—and if you do them then watch your back because they might do you. And if you didn't do them good enough then they'd come back and do you.

'I didn't hate them then. But when I committed my life to the Lord I found I had hatred inside me, and that I could hate. If you're going the Lord's way then all of a sudden you have got love—and you have got hatred as well. Do you understand what I mean?' Paddy asked. 'Before I didn't feel any of that...'

I nodded. 'You've come alive!' 'Yes,' he said. 'All of a sudden "Bang!"—like a volcano going off. All those feelings—hatred and love, desperation, loneliness. I went to the Christian Union at Magdalen College and gave my testimony to them. I told them about my past life—what I've told you. And afterwards one person asked me what was the best thing and the worst thing in my life. And the worst thing in my whole life was when I became a Christian! It was the hardest year of my life, and I've been through hell on earth and back...'

'Because of the pain?' I asked, 'and because you started hurting?' 'Yes', he said. 'The only feelings I had before were physical—but you have emotions inside you that you should have had when you were a child. But you couldn't have them then and they got stuck.'

Paddy has lost touch with his girlfriend Kim and their child, and I wondered if he ever thought of getting in touch again. 'Quite a few times,' he said, 'but I think my bridges are burnt. I'll wait until he's older. Then I'll get in contact—and maybe he'll understand.'

But Paddy prays for Kim and their child. 'I didn't,' he said, 'not until one Mothering Sunday when I had started to come to the service. It was before I had committed myself to the Lord, but I found myself praying. The young kiddies were bringing in daffodils for their mums, and I found myself praying for my ex-girlfriend that she'd have a really good and happy Mothering Sunday. And I burst into tears. I hadn't cried in ten years. Not since my dad died.

'That's one of the biggest problems. I'm not in control. When they say you're born again, with me it literally is born again.'

Dave Bilbrough's song based on 2 Corinthians 5:17 sums up what it is like for Paddy to live his new life—born again of the Holy Spirit of God. Paddy is called Martin now—the name he was given at his baptism. When Martin sings this song—along with all the other people in the service who have been forgiven and given a new life—he sings it with a lot of feeling.

I am a new creation,
No more in condemnation,
Here in the grace of God I stand.
My heart is overflowing,
My love just keeps on growing,
Here in the grace of God I stand.

And I will praise You Lord,
Yes I will praise You Lord,
And I will sing of all that You have done.

A joy that knows no limit,
A lightness in my spirit,
Here in the grace of God I stand.

Dave Bilborough © Thankyou Music 1983

Therefore, if anyone is in Christ, he is a new creation; the old has gone, the new has come! All this is from God, who reconciled us to himself through Christ and gave us the ministry of reconciliation: that God was reconciling the world to himself in Christ, not counting men's sins against them. And he has committed to us the message of reconciliation. We are therefore Christ's ambassadors, as though God were making his appeal through us. We implore you on Christ's behalf: Be reconciled to God. God made him who had no sin to be sin for us, so that in him we might become the righteousness of God.

2 Corinthians 5:17–21

VALUE ME

Many of us believe with our minds that God loves us but have trouble believing it in our hearts. We can't accept that we are liked by him, that we are precious in his sight. Perhaps the negative things that others have said to us in the past have left us believing that we are no good and that we can never be any good.

Perhaps we have a very distorted image of what our heavenly Father is like due to an earthly father who never told us he loved us, never touched us with affection, or even worse, hurt us physically.

I believe God is longing to release our hearts to receive the truth of how much he loves us, how much we are valued by him, are indeed beautiful to him. He is the perfect Father whose desire is to hold his children in his arms, even though he has to discipline his children and clean them up.

Value me

Tell me I'm valued, tell me I'm loved
And the child within my heart will cry
'Who wants a reject?
Who really cares
For a victim of self-hatred and fear?'
A river damned, a stagnant pool,
Enclosed by death, polluted by sin.
Still find me special? Still call me loved?
For my heart finds it hard to accept
You value me.

Tell me I'm needed, respected, affirmed,
And the child within my heart will say,
'How can you value, how can you love
A captive locked in walls of clay?'
A fountain dry, a garden sealed
And overgrown with thorn and weed.
You tell me I'm special, You tell me I'm loved,
Yet I still find it hard to accept
You value me.

Is it deception, or is it a mask
Created by the power of lies?
If I'm forgiven, if it's the truth,
It will only take one glance of Your eyes
And You'll steal my heart, You'll make me whole;
Replacing my old heart of stone.
Please tell me I'm special, please tell me I'm loved
And my heart shall be free to accept;
My heart shall be free to accept
You value me, You value me, You value me.

Phil Lawson Johnston © Cloud Music 1994

Sonia Hall is a Christian and a counsellor, and in training for the ordained ministry. She looks after the pastoral care at a busy parish church and supervises and manages a team of eight lay pastors.

Day after day, people come to see her who are suffering from a lack of value and self-worth. Many of them also have a deep sense of disappointment with God—feeling that somehow he has failed them, and that life just hasn't turned out as they had hoped and believed that it would. Their lack of value seems to manifest itself in different ways, and seems to be different in men and women.

'In men,' Sonia said, 'in the culture in which we live, it manifests itself in workaholism. Men don't feel of value in their own right. So they work harder and harder to attain what they perceive to be value.

Who they are, and the value they have, is related to success.

'In women it can manifest itself when they have children. They can suffer from such a total lack of confidence that they can't even drive a car.'

I wondered what the connection was between having children and losing confidence. Sonia explained. 'A lot of women who have careers don't realize that is where their identity and their value are coming from. Sometimes at dinner parties I'll ask a person what she does, and she will tell me, "I'm just a housewife..." I can see in her eyes what she's feeling, because with the loss of status there comes the loss of self-esteem. If you spend your day changing nappies and feeding children, nobody values that very much; and if what you do doesn't have any value then you don't have any value either.

'People feel like that because of the way we bring up our children. If there is a discrepancy between what we say as a parent, and what we do, and between what we say as a person, and what we do, then people will always hear what we do. If we are very keen on what our children achieve, then, even if we say to them, "I love you whether you achieve or not," we shan't convince them. What they will hear us saying is, "You are of value if you *do* achieve. You are of value if you go to *this* school; if you achieve *that* grade; and if you achieve certain social activities." In terms of self-image it works like clockwork.'

For Sonia, this sort of damage wasn't only being done in families. It was also being done in the Church.

'What we say from the pulpit doesn't always square with the way we live,' she said. 'The preachers tell us that we are of value regardless of what we do and what we are. But if they really value their children, and value other people, for the same things that the rest of the world values them for, then that's what their listeners are going to hear.'

Sonia also has to deal with the damage done from the pulpit in churches where there is a tremendous emphasis on doctrinal purity, and on what is perceived as the Calvinist doctrine of total depravity.

'It tells us that everything we touch we make dirty,' she said, 'and that we have ruined everything in our life. It's "worm" theology, and it says to everyone, "You are a terrible, miserable sinner." But for most people that's the last thing they need to hear. They know it already. What they really need to hear is that God loves them.'

I wondered if Sonia had any problems with the 'prayer of humble access' in the communion service, where we tell God that 'we are not worthy so much as to gather up the crumbs under your table'. I don't like it at all, because I don't believe that any child would talk to its mother or father like that when it sat down to a meal with them— and if it did then there would be something severely wrong with the parent-child relationship.

But Sonia can in fact use the prayer quite happily when she leads a service because she knows what she means by it. 'Before a holy God,' she said, 'we are unworthy in the sense of having sinful attitudes, and behaving sinfully. God is awesome in his holiness, and I think it is right that we approach his throne of grace with reverence and humility.

'However, I do not believe that we are "unworthy" in the sense of being worthless. We have great worth in the sense of being valued according to the price someone is prepared to pay for us. Jesus gave his life for us—and in that sense we are priceless.'

But the pulpit can be the source of healing as well as harming, and Sonia has seen people transformed by what has been said there.

'I have heard Selwyn Hughes preach on Isaiah 43,' she said, 'and he has expounded the word of God with the anointing of the Spirit in such a way that people have really heard that they are valuable in God's eyes. They hear God saying to them, 'You are precious and honoured in my sight . . . I love you'—and they have believed it.

A person's lack of value can often be traced back to the fact that their parents never affirmed them—or they harmed them emotionally or physically. 'James Dobson has written a very good book called *Hide and Seek*,' said Sonia, 'and he points out that even a child in its pram will pick up the affirmation which comes because of what the child looks like. If it looks good, people will make a fuss of it. If it doesn't, they won't. So parents need to be taught how to affirm in other ways—and they do need to be taught.

'If you say to a child, "I love you," but then you go to a church meeting rather than play tiddlywinks, the child will hear you saying that church meetings are more important than she is. And if that happens day after day, then that's what she's going to believe.

'The child psychologist Donald Winnicott spoke about "good enough mothering". He taught that none of us can be perfect, and he said that it is better to be a good enough parent than it is to be perfect. Because the world is full of imperfect situations.'

Someone once said to Sonia, 'Let's face it, we've all done irretrievable damage to our children.' 'And it's true,' Sonia said, 'we have. So where we've sinned let's repent, and put that in the past, and then do what we can to put it right. It may be that as fathers and mothers we need to do some work to sort out what we really value, and whether we are putting pressure on our children.'

I wondered how parents could value their teenage children when they were behaving appallingly and being almost unbelievably rude—and how the child (who was presumably behaving like that for some reason) might still feel valued.

'There isn't a straight correlation,' Sonia said. 'But I have observed in professional people, and in Christian professional people, that there is a correlation between children doing that as teenagers and the amount of quality time that the children are given as children, and the amount of unconditional love. What James Dobson says is, "Parents, hang in there, and just get them through it somehow!"

'Somehow parents have to go on loving—and go on being there. But with boundaries. Because children actually enjoy boundaries. They feel more valued when they have them. They need to be children, and it is my observation that children who call their parents by their Christian names may be more likely to be difficult.'

I asked Sonia how things could be put right for the person who didn't feel valued? 'It is a lifetime's job,' she said. 'Keys can be turned instantly, and doors can be opened. But the work has to go on for a lifetime.

'Mary Pytches says that what happens in the future depends on what we do in the present with our past. So we come to a point where we say, "Yes, I have been damaged. I wasn't affirmed. I don't feel that I've got much value." Then we go on from there. We say, "Right, I accept at a deep level that this happened to me. But now I am going to ask God to change me. I am going to take some risks." '

When Sonia is working with people she gets them to meditate on aspects of God's word that convey how much we are loved—irrespective of what we do.

'There is a form of therapy,' she said, 'which is based on the assumption that we feel the way we do because of our belief system. If I brought my domestic cat in here and put it on the floor, you would probably feel quite safe. But if I went to the wildlife park and got a wild cat, a tiger, and brought that in here then you would feel fear. Because your belief system is that a domestic cat won't hurt you, but the big cat will.

'One theory of depression is that a person who is depressed has a negative view of the world, of the future, and of themselves. But if you can help them to change the way they think about themselves—and they are in fact changed by the way they think—then you can change their mood. That has been researched, and there is very good evidence for it.

'If someone asks, "What am I worth?" Christianity has the answer: "You are worth more than the whole world." Once people start to think about themselves differently then they will start to feel different. They will be transformed as they change their minds—and I believe that the Holy Spirit of God can change us. But it is a lifetime's work.'

How we can change

What Sonia says about thinking differently about ourselves is the key to unlocking a whole new world. But it isn't a new truth. The Apostle Paul knew about it, and in the letter he wrote to the Christians in Rome he told them to 'be transformed by the renewing of your mind' (Romans 12:2).

Our mind is full of information. Billions and billions of pieces of information. But some of that information is wrong. Some of it was programmed into us when we were too young to disagree with it or to check it out for accuracy—and the sheer smallness and help-lessness of a baby can make it feel inferior if it doesn't receive an enormous amount of tenderness and loving.

As the child grows up it can be given other pieces of false information. 'White people are inferior'—or 'Black people are inferior.' 'Women are inferior—and their purpose in life is to look after other people'—or 'Men are inferior—they lack compassion and understanding.'

Some of the words that our parents speak to us can burn into our brains like molten iron. Mary's father told her that she was useless and hopeless—and until she came to the turning point in her life she believed it (her story is in chapter 6).

My own mother's nickname for me was 'Bandy'—because my legs are slightly bandy. Because of that I spent most of my life believing that my legs were ugly. I only started to accept them when I was listening to a meditation on a cassette by the Cowley Father, Christopher Bryant.

Part of the meditation consisted in being still in the presence of God, and being aware of all the different parts of my own body. I began with my head and worked my way down. But when I got to my legs I burst into tears. I realized that for the whole of my life I had hated them, because I saw them as ugly. Then I thanked God for them, and for the reliable way they have carried me round since the day that I started to walk (quite early, when I was nine months old, which may account for them being very slightly bowed). At a deep level I accepted them as they are—and told them I liked them.

That may sound a strange sort of transaction, but it worked. There are many people who see themselves as ugly who are not ugly—and it often stems from parental criticism or so-called teasing. That feeling of ugliness is why people undergo plastic surgery—because they want to change their nose, or their ears, or some other part of their anatomy.

If we have been believing something that isn't true then we can change. In some ways our brain is like a computer, and we can reprogram it with correct information. White people are not inferior—and black people are not inferior. Every human being is made in the image and likeness of God, and everyone is equally precious and valuable.

We can change our minds by putting the correct information into them. The old, wrong information will still be there—and sometimes we shall hear it playing inside our heads like an old tape that we used to listen to over and over again. Saying to us 'You're worthless', or 'You're useless', or 'You're hopeless', or 'You're ugly.' Then we have to contradict the old message and tell it the truth. It is the truth that will set us free—so we need to know the right words to correct the wrong words.

'I am not worthless—I am worth more than the whole world. I know that because Jesus said so.'

'I am not useless—God will fulfil his purpose for me—and he has got one!'

'I am not hopeless—"Praised be the God and Father of our Lord Jesus Christ! In his great mercy by the resurrection of Jesus Christ from the dead, he gave us [which includes me!] new birth into a living hope, the hope of an inheritance, reserved in heaven [for us], which nothing can destroy or spoil or wither" (1 Peter 1:3–4, REB).'

One of the best ways to be transformed by the renewing of our mind is to listen to Christian words set to music, and that is why there is a music cassette to accompany this book.

Transformed by love

Jo used to feel useless and worthless—but now she has a lovely sense of her own worth and value in Christ. The feelings that she used to have came to the surface one day in a workshop on creative writing that I was running at my church. There was a weekend of workshops and worship, and Phil Lawson Johnston and Helen Kucharek were running it.

At the creative writing workshop people had to work—and to write. Up to 200 words on set subjects—and after each one was finished I invited them to read out what they had written. The standard was very high—and some of the things that people wrote about were very moving.

But one person didn't want to read out what she had written. Jo held her notebook protectively in her arms, and said, 'No! I can't possibly read it out ... it's no good!' She said that laughingly—but inside she felt far more like crying. A little later on, however, she agreed to share her writing with us:

'Just after my second birthday I was playing outside, climbing on a heavy wooden bench, when it toppled on top of me.

'I was rushed to hospital where I was taken away from my parents, screaming with agony and also because they had left me. They weren't allowed to see me for forty-eight hours, because those were the rules in those days.

'After that, they were allowed to visit me for half an hour every day. Every day when the bell rang for visitors to go home I would turn my little head away from my parents, knowing that they were going. I think probably that I thought life was always going to be like that.

'This memory has stayed with me all my life. I remember the agony, and also feeling bereft because my parents had deserted me. It took me many years to get over this incident.'

In the next exercise (which was to write not more than 200 words on an incident which had triggered a particular emotion in people—happiness, sadness, desolation, joy or whatever), Jo wrote about what she had felt like when she didn't want to read out her writing:

'I felt just now an emotion I haven't felt for a long time. I lived with this emotion for many years. Perhaps it followed on from my stay in hospital. Afer that I became fearful, timid and withdrawn. This continued at school.

'I always felt so useless and worthless. It seemed I was no good at anything. To make matters worse I was teased by the children, and made to feel even more hopeless by the teacher. I can remember many incidents when I was made to look a fool in class. Maybe that's what I was.

'Just now, those feelings of being useless and worthless came back. I didn't want to show myself up as a fool. I wanted to opt out, to give up. "I can't do it," I thought, "I can't do anything right." I felt so completely and utterly inadequate I actually wanted to cry, and felt tears prick my eyes. But then I would have looked even more of a fool, so I fought them back . . .

'I am so thankful that God loves me as I am. With him I am never a fool. I am loved and accepted unconditionally. To him I am not worthless, useless or hopeless, and I am so grateful to him for loving me for what I am. He makes me feel so happy. In God I have found someone who understands me so completely, and in him I have found my security, my greatest love, my greatest treasure.'

A child can suffer a terrible sense of dereliction if it feels abandoned, and the feeling can stay with it for the rest of its life—like an aching wound inside that never goes away. And the effect of bullying on a child can be crippling. David was bullied at school (you can read about it in chapter 5), and so was Jo.

After the workshop was over, she told me how she now came to have this deep awareness of her own worth and value in Christ—after so many years of feelng worthless and useless.

'After I broke my leg my parents did everything they could to try and give me confidence. But when I started school, which was my first primary school, I was still a very frightened, fearful little girl. Very timid, and very shy. Also, I think I was quite slow to learn, because I was off sick a lot with tonsillitis, which meant that the learning was a very slow process.

'At the end of term they used to have a morning when all the parents came, and we all had to stand in a row with what we'd achieved that term, which was our stars. Gold stars for very, very good. Silver stars for very good. Red stars for good. Blue stars for trying, and so on. The worst colours were green and brown. And always at the bottom of the row there was me—with just three stars, two brown and one green. I had to stand there—exposed as being useless and a failure in front of all the mummies and daddies and in front of all the other children.

'Because I did so badly at school and because I was so shy and timid they used to pick on me—and I found it very hard to make friends. There was just one person at that stage of my life, other than my parents, who actually accepted me—and she was my very, very best friend. She lived opposite to us and we had a lovely relationship. But when I was nine she moved up to Newcastle with her parents and I was devastated. I had lost my one friend who liked and accepted me.

'The headmistress of my primary school was an ogre. I remember her threatening me with the cane for not knowing my two times table. My self-esteem was knocked further and further down because of the way they treated me. They made me feel a nothing. A complete failure.

'They were constantly showing me up as a fool and showing me up as hopeless. In class they would send me outside if I didn't know the answer to something—they never sent me outside the door for being naughty. So I actually missed a lot of the lessons because I was standing outside. I didn't tell my parents about this until some time later, and when they heard they were furious. But by then it was too late, because I'd left.

'Because I'd been so unhappy, my parents moved me to another school a bit early. That headmistress was very charming, but she wasn't really a very nice person. It was a private school and a lot of the girls came from very wealthy homes. Some were very spoilt. I think I was unlucky in my class. Because even when I first started in the school I was picked on. I suppose it was my whole demeanor. They thought I was feeble because I'd been so knocked down confidence-wise at my other school. And I was easy to pick on because I was so timid and I thought so little of myself. Other children love that.

'So I had a problem with the girls accepting me—although I did in the end have a friend. I'm not quite sure why she was my friend, because she was a funny sort of friend. She was nasty to me at the same time.

'At that school I had a maths teacher who was horrible. She used to throw books and board rubbers at me because I couldn't do things right. She used to call me useless and stupid the whole time.

After a couple of years she gave up on me. She'd go round the whole class asking questions and leave me out. So I wasn't learning anything. She would just totally ignore me.

'At the same school there was a prefect who picked on me horribly as well. She was my house captain and she found out that I wasn't earning any points for the house. One day after a house meeting she reduced me to tears. I can't remember the exact conversation, because it's a long time ago. But she told me that I was hopeless and pathetic and that I had to do better. She made me take my books up to her every Friday to the sixth-formers' room and she would pick holes in my work. She'd go through it and say, "That's disgusting!" and "That's no good, you're not trying hard enough." But I really was.

'So at that school I was knocked down even more. My parents pulled me out when I was twelve and sent me to a much nicer school where I got on a lot better and where I was very happy. I got on very well with the girls and the teachers were wonderful. They encouraged me, and brought me out of my shell—although the hurts from the past were still there.

'I left school and did a secretarial training, because I didn't know what else I could do, and again I had a horrible teacher. I learned shorthand and typing and I wasn't much good at that either. I couldn't get my speed up. I remember having to go and see the principal because my work wasn't up to standard, and being told I was going to be thrown out unless I improved my speeds and improved my work. Finally I left with reasonable speeds, but I went on to do another month's training at another college to improve my speeds.

'Then I became a secretary in London. But I'm not a very efficient person and secretarial work wasn't really the right career for me. I like to be with people. Helping them, understanding their problems, and caring for them. I probably should have been something like a nurse. But I was a secretary—and I was in a series of disastrous jobs.

'I had an Italian woman boss in one of my first jobs, with a fiery temper, and she was horrible. I seemed to go from one place to another where I was picked on and made to feel hopelessly inadequate. That woman actually demoted me in the end, and, because I was so unhappy, I left. In the end I did find a job where I was very happy. So that was good. But again the memories of all that were still very much with me, and they stayed with me.

'Then I fell in love, and I got married, and had children. I had always dreamed of getting married and having children, because I thought to myself, "Well, I'm obviously not going to be a really successful secretary, I'm not that sort of material. But I'll get married and I'll become a mum." It was what I really wanted, and I thought it was the one thing I would succeed at.

'But having children is no bed of roses! They are quite hard work, and demanding. And I realized that I wasn't being the wonderful mother that I had always dreamed of being. So I felt that I was failing in the one thing I had always thought I could be good at. After having four children I realized I wasn't coping at all, and my dreams of being this perfect mother were shattered. I was full of self-doubt again.

'I had my first child, a daughter, by Caesarean section. Childbirth wasn't as straightforward as I thought it would be. I couldn't even manage that! I was quite low after the birth, both emotionally and physically, and, when my daughter was a year old, I had an ectopic pregnancy. Unfortunately, this was very badly handled by my doctor, who, even though I was seriously ill, refused to believe it was anything more than my imagination. I was made to feel that I was a neurotic woman and a nuisance, when all the time I was in severe pain and bleeding heavily internally. It wasn't until I nearly died that he finally believed me. I was rushed into hospital, and my baby and my fallopian tube were removed. I was devastated.

'After this I failed to conceive the second child we wanted so much, since the ectopic pregnancy had made me infertile. All my friends were having second babies, and everywhere I looked I saw pregnant women and babies. I felt I had failed my husband in not being able to have a second child.

'Finally, after a series of operations, I was told I had a 25 per cent chance of having a baby. Our prayers were answered when I gave birth to a boy. Then another one eighteen months later, and another one twenty-two months later.

'All this put a great strain on me, and I found after my fourth baby I really wasn't coping. It was like banging a nail into a piece of wood—knock, knock, knock—and I'd been knocked down so low. I was in such a pit that I felt I was never going to get out. It was a pit of my own failure, my unworthiness. I felt I had nothing to give any more. That I was completely and utterly useless. I felt so empty that I had nothing even to give to my family any more. I felt so guilty, too, because I had let everyone down—Nick, and my children. I wasn't the perfect mother I'd hoped I would be. I was hopelessly harassed—and constantly tired and irritable and anxious.

'I would never have taken my own life. But when I was crossing the road or driving I would think, "Well, if anything happens to me, it's not going to matter. I think that maybe everybody would be better off without me." Which was a terrible stage to get to. I felt that I was in a real black pit, spiralling down.

'It was at this point that I went to the parish house party at Ashburnham, where James Jones was speaking. They had a lovely service on the Saturday evening and then somebody had a word of knowledge, saying that a person there was carrying a lot of bitterness around with them. Which I was. I was carrying a lot of hurt around, but I was also carrying a lot of bitterness. Because in some ways the hurt had turned to bitterness. I didn't know whether the word of knowledge was really for me, but it spoke to me. So did the whole service, and it meant a lot to me.

'There was a sketch in it about somebody carrying loads of cases and baggage, and the message was that we should let Jesus carry all our baggage and give it to him. At that point I became aware of all the baggage I'd been carrying around with me for years and years. All the hurts of my childhood. I suppose I had resented my past. I resented the way I'd been treated at school. There was hurt and there was worthlessness. And anger—anger over everything. Over the way that silly doctor had treated me. Over the way the teachers had treated me. And there was guilt, too, for failing everyone. All that. There was this terrible feeling of failure and worthlessness—but anger was very much there as well, anger even with myself for making such a flop of my life.

'I knew then that God wanted to heal me of all those things from the past—but I knew it wasn't the right time to go up for healing just then.

'But a couple of months later I arranged to see a lady called Joan and a lady called Mary, and I told them much of my past and the things that I felt I needed prayer for, which were my feelings of self-hatred, guilt and hurt. Those feelings had come out through the counselling I'd had. But the counselling didn't work because what I was doing was just wallowing around in the pit of my past and of my hurts. It wasn't lifting me out of them.

'Mary and Joan started to pray. And as they prayed over me I felt this fizz go through me—like a warm tingling sensation of great love. I suppose that was the first time that it had ever hit me that God was real and that he did care for me and that he did value me. And that he loved me and that he really wanted to heal me. The healing began then. I wasn't totally healed. But that was the start of it.

'A little while after that I had a vision of Jesus. I saw him. He didn't speak, but his eyes told me how much he loved me. Then not long after that (when I was blow-drying my hair) God spoke to me. It was the first time God had ever spoken to me in that way, and it was so clear. He said, "You've got to let go." I didn't quite understand. I thought, "I know that was God, but I don't understand what he means." But later on I did.

'This was all happening over a period of six months. Then I was invited to go to a church in Chorleywood with a friend, and there was a talk being given on inner healing by Mary Pytches. It was a lovely talk. She said that each of us has a child inside us, and very often that child is a hurting child. So we have got to let Jesus come and heal the child within us. She talked about the many areas of childhood hurt: abuse, and bullying, and all sorts of hurt. There are so many.

'After that there was a time of prayer ministry. So I went up and stood with a group of people—and some ladies in front of me, when they were prayed for, started weeping and wailing. I wanted to go home at that point and to get out. But there was no exit for me. I couldn't get out. I was stuck there. Finally, when a lady spotted me, and came and started to pray for me, I thought, "Well, I'll close my eyes and look as though I'm praying," which I did. And after a few seconds I felt as if I was being pushed over.

'So I opened one of my eyes and I said to the lady, "Why are you pushing me over?" She said, "I'm not pushing you over. The Holy Spirit is wanting to anoint you." I said "Oh!"—and I closed my eyes again. And again I felt a strong push—this time stronger than the first. I opened my eyes, and I think I was looking a bit frightened. But the lady said, "Don't worry! It's all right. We'll catch you." And she said, "You've got to let go!" Then I remembered those very words that God had given me: "You've got to let go!"

'But it wasn't just referring to this. It was talking about letting go of the past. So I did let go. I let the Holy Spirit push me over—and I let God come to me in his great power and love and mercy. And I received from God in a way that I had never done before. I found myself lying on the floor and I know that I cried. I think I was crying because I suddenly realized how much he loved me. And I realized that he cared for me. And that was just so wonderful. I couldn't believe how he could love me and value me.

'As time went on I had a great feeling of acceptance—and all my self-worth and the value that I have in Christ came to me. That was the changing point for me. That was when God became a real person.

'I received God's love in a very real way, but I also let go of all my hurts and all my feelings of self-hatred and unworthiness. I let go to God—and he took them away. So when I got up I was a different person. I wasn't the old Jo. I was a new Jo. He had given me a new heart. I knew my place in Christ and I knew it deep down within me. It wasn't just head knowledge. I really knew that God loved and valued me.

'From that moment on I didn't only have a new heart. It was strange, but it was as if I had new eyes. I saw everything in a different light. Before I had been so inward looking—and always looking in on myself, and so hurt. But now I had been given new eyes and a new heart, and I was looking out and everything seemed to be so different. I can't explain it. I would look at a field or at flowers, or at the sea or the sky, and there would be some meaning in it all. Everything seemed brighter. And I had a new understanding of people and of God.

'After this my prayer life changed, because it was a real relationship. I was actually praying to somebody who was very close and very precious and very special. There was a real love-relationship.

'I became really hungry and thirsty for God. I longed to be in God's presence. I longed to hear him speak—and he did speak to me. In the evening I would often sit there with my nose in the Bible, because I had this great longing to read it. And all that has never gone, but it has been a bit like the sea. It goes in waves. You get crests. Sometimes it's not so much, and that feeling of real closeness isn't there. But then it comes back again, and I guess that is a normal Christian life, isn't it—that there are peaks and troughs. But I know that I will never be in that pit again, because I have been lifted out of it.

'There's that wonderful Psalm about God lifting us up out of the pit. "I waited patiently for the Lord; he inclined to me and heard my cry. He drew me up from the desolate pit, out of the miry bog. He set my feet upon a rock making my steps secure . . ."—which is what he did. He took me out of that awful pit that I'd been in and set my feet upon secure rock. The rock of Christ. And then it says, "He put a new song in my mouth, a song of praise to our God. Many will see and fear, and put their trust in the Lord" (Psalm 40:3, RSV).

'And he did just that. He gave me a new song, a new heart, and new eyes—and many people will see and fear. And people did see the difference in me—and they saw that it was God. And the glory went to him, because he was the only one who could lift me out of the pit. He's saved me. He was the only way—he is the way, the truth and the life. And that was the only way for healing.'

Jo had certainly been healed—and I could see it in her eyes and in the whole of her. So I asked her why she thought the feeling of worthlessness and uselessness had suddenly overwhelmed her at the workshop on creative writing. She thought for a moment.

'Perhaps it was just the sheer memory—and the feelings of

unworthiness. I thought I shouldn't really be on this course, because I'm not really a very good creative writer at all. And perhaps that brought those memories back.'

'Was it like being back at school again,' I suggested, 'when you had that feeling of being exposed in front of everybody?' 'Yes,' she said, 'it was. I was going to have to expose myself and look a fool. And I didn't want to do that. But great blessing has come from it, hasn't it? It's amazing how God can use something. And he has healed me ...'

'Yes,' I said, 'and healing's like salvation ... with three tenses, in the past and the present and the future. I have been saved, I am being saved and I will be saved. And you have been healed, and you are being healed, and you will be healed. But it hardly ever happens overnight.'

Jo agreed. 'Yes,' she said. 'It's a very gradual process. Because our lives are very complex and we are constantly being changed—from one degree of glory to another. And all the time God is bringing up areas in our lives that need to be changed and to be healed. He's still changing me. But I can't look back. I look forward. And I look to Jesus and keep my eyes fixed on him.

'There are times when I suddenly cry out, "Help! I'm hopeless! I can't cope!" Maybe when the children are being particularly naughty, and I'll feel that as a mother I've done wrong and I've failed them. Or times like that Saturday, when the feelings came back. But I just have to remember the promises that God has given to me. I can look back on what he's done for me already and look forward to what he's going to do.'

'And what he's doing in the now,' I said, 'because you're not just living in the past and in the future—you're living a very rich life in the present.' 'Yes,' said Jo, 'and life would not be normal if there were not ups and downs, and peaks and troughs. But I have something now that I can hold on to which I never had before. Sometimes I have to cling on for dear life. I have bad weeks—and good weeks. But that rock is always there.'

Jo believes it is enormously important to build on the good and to affirm children. 'I would never claim to be a perfect mother,' she said. 'I'm learning all the time. And as the children change and grow up and develop so their needs change. But one thing I know that is really, really important to me: looking back on my past, and the damage that was done by people who criticized me so destructively and knocked me down to make me feel so useless, the one thing that has come out of that is that with my own children I feel it is so very, very important to encourage and build up all the good things in them and never to be harsh or critical or to pull them down and make them feel useless. Always to make them feel that they have value and self-worth and to know that they are loved and accepted despite their bad points, which of course they do have.'

'Even when they're naughty?' I asked. 'Even when they're naughty, yes,' said Jo. 'They have to know that they are loved and accepted. I get very upset if I hear about people or see people putting children down and making them feel useless. Whether it be by other children bullying them or by parents who have made their children feel useless and worthless.

'And so much can be said with words. A child can be continuously told that they are stupid, or pathetic, or hopeless, or whatever. And it's so damaging. If you keep saying these things they begin to think that they are. But you have to build them up in love and not destroy them. If you destroy the child you destroy the person that they are going to become, because our childhoods affect the whole of our lives and the whole of our personalities. But God came into the world in order to heal us—and he can heal the child within us, however great the hurt has been.

'Looking back, I was chained down by my past. The chains held me back from receiving the love of God, the love that he longs to pour out on each one of us, that is ours in Christ. The chains held me back from giving God all of me, and worshipping him in Spirit and in truth.

'I couldn't believe he wanted all of me anyway, or that he wanted to give his love to me. But all I had to do was to call out to him from the darkness of my pit, and he was there— tenderly in his great love and mercy lifting me out and setting my feet upon a rock.

'My chains were broken and I was free. He put a new song on my

47

lips and he gave me a new heart. I had never realized before how great his love is for us and how precious we are to him. I am still learning how broad and how long, how high and how deep, is God's love for us in Christ, and how nothing in all of creation can separate us from that love.

'Jesus came to set the captives free—and so many of us are captives of our own past. Jesus longs to set us free from the chains that hold us. Jesus is the truth, and it is the truth that sets us free.'

> Now to him who is able to do immeasurably more than all we ask or imagine . . . to him be glory in the church and in Christ Jesus throughout all generations, for ever and ever. Amen.
>
> Ephesians 3:20–21

3

TELL ME I'M LOVED

Phil's song *Value Me* starts with a request: 'Tell me I'm valued, tell me I'm loved.' That is what every human being most wants to know and most wants to be true. That they are greatly valued and greatly loved.

But if no one ever tells us that we are loved, or shows us how much they value us, then we shall start to pretend that we don't care. We shall grow hard shells outside ourselves to protect the vulnerable person inside us—and our hearts will grow cold, because the warmth and the fire of love have never touched them.

If we want to know that we are valued and loved, then we shall have to allow the Spirit of God to change us and transform us. We were looking at the process of transformation in the last chapter, and we saw how it starts with changing our minds. 'Go on being transformed by the renewing of your minds' St Paul wrote to the Christians in Rome (Romans 12:2), and the tense of the verb is the present continuous—used to describe something that goes on happening. The transformation of our mind is a process, and so is our transformation into the likeness of Christ.

Paul wrote about that to the Christians in Corinth: 'We, who ... contemplate the Lord's glory, are being transformed into his likeness, with ever-increasing glory, which comes from the Lord, who is the Spirit' (2 Corinthians 3:18).

Contemplation and contemplative prayer are something that most of us have to learn, but they are one of the ways in which we can let the love of God penetrate deep into our hearts. But we sometimes have to be desperate before we will turn to this sort of prayer.

David Huggett's story

David Huggett is discovering contemplative prayer, but it hasn't been easy for him. He has found it very difficult and very hard to stop being the rector of a successful parish and live a very different sort of life in Cyprus. Added to that, he says that he seems to be defined now as 'Joyce Huggett's husband'.

People seem to speak to him in the way that the evil spirit spoke to the seven sons of Sceva, who were trying unsuccessfully to cast it out: 'Jesus I know; and Paul I know; but who are you?' (Acts 19:15, RSV). People seem to be saying to David, 'Joyce Huggett I know . . . but who are you?' I asked David to tell me what that felt like.

'Back in Britain,' he said, 'when I was rector of a church, I was a person with a ministry and some sort of track record. I had that because of my work. But here in Cyprus very few people have heard about me. Obviously they haven't—because nobody hears about a parish priest working in Nottingham. But over twenty years in Nottingham I had come to be known and appreciated. I felt that as a person I was appreciated for who I was and what I did.

'When a couple come into a place as missionaries usually both of them would be totally unknown. But Joyce has an international reputation. People have read her books out here—as indeed they have all over the world. So she was known. And I was unknown.

'Twenty years ago Joyce hadn't written anything—so when we went to Nottingham I was the curate who had come from Cambridge and she was the curate's wife. But now the tables are reversed. Since we have come to Cyprus it's more like, "Joyce we know very well—and David is her husband but we hardly know anything about him."

'How does that feel? In my worst moments I feel I have lost an awful lot. I suppose I must feel like every woman who feels that she is simply an appendage to a known person. And that is what I do feel. When time is empty and there isn't much going on it can feel that people are writing to us because they know Joyce—and that people are asking both of us to do things simply because they know Joyce.

'At some conferences people have said, "Oh, it's so good to meet David, and find there's a real person behind Joyce." I know that has been every woman's lot in past generations—and I am deeply sorrowful that we have treated women like that. I understand now something of the woman's lot—of being known simply as the husband's wife.

'In my best moments I am the chief fan of my wife. I love her success. I am thrilled by what she has done. And if it is true that in order that she may increase I have to decrease then that's OK, because the balance has been the other way for a long time, and I am very happy and very thrilled with her success.

'Every time people acknowledge her I say, "Well, that's my wife! And I'm proud of her." So there's no problem there—or there isn't in the good times . . .

'When you find yourself in a totally new situation it is as if God is pouring you from one vessel into another. And that's good. We can get too settled. Jeremiah talks about someone who has "settled on his lees," or who is "like wine left on its dregs, not poured from one jar to another" (Jeremiah 48:11, RSV and NIV).

'I know that a new situation is an enormous challenge and a good opportunity to grow. So that coming to Cyprus and not being known is a marvellous opportunity to grow in new gifting and new abilities. I am excited by that. But it isn't the same for both of us. The change is big for Joyce as well as for me, but she has brought her writing with her. We are not both struggling at the bottom to grow again.

'So on the one hand I really can say that for me to start again is an exciting adventure with God. But I am finding that it is also full of pain and difficulty. I have many days when I don't have work to do as I would have had back in Nottingham.

'In a parish there is always ongoing work to do. You go into a busy situation, and you work, and then you go home. But sometimes here there isn't much to do at all, and it is in those times that I have to learn, and to say, "This is the time of growth. This is when I learn to be quiet and to be still, and to read and to grow." And that's hard.

'One of the reasons why it's so hard is that Joyce still has her writing, and sometimes I feel alone in the adventure. I know that it's a good experience to learn what it is to grow alone. But it's costly and it's painful.

'Sometimes I wish my chief love was writing letters. Joyce loves writing letters and she loves writing books. But that's not my love. My love is people, and to be cut off from people is hard.

'It throws me back on questions like, "Will I survive, or will I not? Will I crack up—or will I slightly fall apart?" It is sometimes hard not to be busy, and not to have anything to do, and to be still. But it's a very important lesson. And if I can learn to be still and to be alone, and not to find my value in what I do, but to begin to find it more in just being, that's important.

'The growth in silence and solitude which came with my exploration of contemplative prayer have begun to help me with that. It's not quite so scary now to be alone with no agenda, but just to be.

'There seems to be a sort of parallel in the life of Jesus to what I feel has happened in my life. At the start, his ministry was to preach, teach, heal and love the common people, and to win over the religious people. I believe that he meant his ministry to achieve these things, and he worked really hard at it. But then a time came when there was a dramatic change, when scripture says that he withdrew to be beyond Jordan. He realized that a lot of the people only came for the bread and the miracles. They came because there were goodies, and the religious people had turned against him.

'Then Jesus almost totally gave up that ministry, and he simply shut himself down to going to the cross and dying. He handed over what he came to do to those who would follow him. The ministry to the people and the ministry to the religious leaders would have to be done by the disciples.

'I believe that Jesus must have had a tremendous feeling of bereavement at that time in his life. As if he was saying, "Well, the people aren't going to follow me and believe in me, and in all my miracles and teaching. They are just forgetting it and coming for the good things. And the religious people whō I've spent hours trying to win over are so blind and so besotted with their narrowness that they won't listen." So Jesus left all that ministry, and he walked into the loneliness of simply going to die.

'I know that he came in order to die, but there was that point at which apparently all he had done had to be left behind. It seems to me that when I walked out on what I did in the past—into a new place—it was like a death. The the death of one ministry and the birth of a new one.

'I don't believe that it was a foolish thing to do, although other people might say that it was. One of my problems is that I can be tempted to think that people are saying, "David's lost his bottle," or, "He's gone for the sun in Cyprus: it's a nice life, and he ought to be here running a big church. That's what he's good at, but he's gone soft."

'I wonder sometimes what Jesus felt when he gave up his public ministry. When he no longer went about among them openly, and just gave himself to go to the cross. I believe that what I have done is probably the best thing I have ever done in my life. But it's not easy. It's hard.'

That was the point at which David finished telling me his story. But the growth and the change and the struggle are still going on. In the book of Revelation the risen Christ makes a promise to those who are having a struggle.

> Him who overcomes I will make a pillar in the temple of my God. Never again will he leave it. I will write on him the name of my God and the name of the city of my God, the new Jerusalem, which is coming down out of heaven from my God; and I will also write on him my new name.
>
> Revelation 3:12

Martin Ingleby's story

David Huggett is having his struggle, and is on his particular journey. Other people are having different struggles, and on different journeys. When I checked in at Gatwick to go to Cyprus for a retreat led by David and Joyce Huggett, I noticed two wheelchairs at the next desk. A man was in one of them and a woman in the other. As I went past them to get some coffee before the flight, I wondered what sort of struggle they were going to have to get on to their flight. They had two young women with them, obviously there to help them, but as I walked through the airport I found myself thinking about what it must be like to be confined to a wheelchair.

In Cyprus I was able to find out just a little of what it was like—because both the people I had seen at Gatwick were on the retreat—Martin and Susan Ingleby. Martin agreed to give me an interview for *Value Me*, and I began by asking him how long ago he had been taken ill.

'It was in 1946,' he told me. 'I was in the army, in the Coldstream Guards, out in Cairo just after the war, and I got polio there. I was twenty-one. To start with it was pretty bad. I couldn't move anything except my head—and I could only move that a little. Then, gradually, my top half recovered, but not below the waist. I wasn't in an iron lung, but they thought my life was in danger. For some time I was entirely helpless.'

I asked Martin what it felt like to be incapacitated in the way that he was. 'Well, it came over me quite slowly,' he said, 'which was a very good thing. If I had realized all of a sudden what it was going to be like, it would have been a great shock. I was in hospital for eighteen months, and in that time I realized there were still considerable possibilities.'

'Did you get married after your illness?' I asked. 'Yes,' he said. 'I went to Oxford first, then I started reading for the Bar (Susan insisted on it) and we were married about a year after that, by the Bishop of Rochester, Dr Chavasse. We had five children. We lost our son nearly twenty years ago. Now we have four daughters and six grandchildren.'

I wondered when Martin Ingleby had become a Christian, and how it had happened. 'It was in 1956,' he said, 'through a school friend, John Bickersteth. I knew him fairly well at Eton but I hadn't seen him for years. Then we just happened to meet at a cocktail party, and I think he sensed that I was wondering about the things of God. Possibly whether to be ordained or not. And he asked me if I'd like him to come round, so that we could read the Bible together.

'That sounded a very shocking idea to me! Very un-English! And I was rather surprised to find somebody who obviously took the

Bible seriously and was prepared to believe what it said. So, rather reluctantly, I agreed. And John was wonderful. He must have been very busy, because he was a curate at Sanderstead at the time, but he came up several times and we sat on the sofa and read the Bible together in our London flat.

'As I result of that I made a great effort to kneel down (which I can't do now), and I asked the Lord to come into my life. It was about the same time that Billy Graham was over here at Wembley, and as an act of witness I went forward at Wembley. That was quite an undertaking, because it is an enormous place. I walked a little bit on crutches in those days, and I managed to get down on to the grass, and then walk all the way back again. I was glad I did.'

'Did it make a difference to be a Christian?' I asked. 'Very much so,' Martin said. 'I suppose the most obvious outward difference was that I started going to Stewards' Trust meetings in London. I wasn't one of the people who started them, but I came in fairly early on and we used to have evangelistic meetings in people's drawing rooms from time to time, and also regular Bible studies. We used to go to All Souls, Langham Place, which at that time had John Stott as the Rector, and John Lefroy and John Collins were there as well. Those are the most obvious outward differences—but I hope it showed in every part of my life.'

'What about inside differences?' I wanted to know. 'There is a sense in which you, from your own social background, must have had quite a sense of being a person of value in the world's eyes. You went to the top school. You've got a title. You've got an estate. They're all lovely things to have. But have you got an additional sense of worth now because you're a Christian—an additional sense of value added to those things that the world counts as precious and would like to have?'

'Yes, I have,' said Martin. 'All those things I am very grateful for—and I regard them as an opportunity given by God, but most important of all is the realization that I am precious in the sight of God, and that he sent his Son to die for me. And remember that he chose his disciples—they didn't choose him. And he has chosen me. I have to remind myself that he seems to go in for choosing

The righteous cry out, and the Lord hears them;
he delivers them from all their troubles.
The Lord is close to the broken-hearted
and saves those who are crushed in spirit.

Psalm 34:17–18

'O Jerusalem, Jerusalem, you who kill the
prophets and stone those sent to you, how often I
have longed to gather your children together, as
a hen gathers her chicks under her wings, but you
were not willing!'

Luke 13:34

'When Israel was a child, I loved him, and out of
Egypt I called my son. But the more I called
Israel, the further they went from me. They
sacrificed to the Baals and they burned incense to
images. It was I who taught Ephraim to walk,
taking them by the arms; but they did not realise
it was I who healed them. I led them with cords of
human kindness, with ties of love; I lifted the yoke
from their neck and bent down to feed them . . .
How can I give you up, Ephraim? How can I hand
you over, Israel? . . . My heart is changed within
me; all my compassion is aroused.

Hosea 11:1–4, 8

more of the weak things of this world than he does of the strong—and to realize therefore that he has a purpose for me; and for everyone.'

I asked Martin to tell me what the particular difficulties were that he had to grapple with because of his disability. 'Well, the physical difficulties are quite great,' he said. 'For example, I can't have a bath here because I can't get out of the bath. Then there's the difficulty that everything takes several times longer, so one's time is much more limited. And since Susan got ill five years ago I have to do a lot of the things that she can't do. All the telephoning and all the letter writing. We have to have quite a number of domestic staff because Susan needs someone around most of the time, and I have to do most of the communicating.

'Also, we have got quite a big estate. It is mostly heather, and a lot of forestry and a number of small farms. We have a part-time agent, but there are still a lot of things that can't be left to the agent which fall on me and Susan.

'I used to attend the House of Lords fairly regularly, but now I only attend once or twice a fortnight. I can't take an active part because I simply haven't got the time to do the homework. Since Susan became ill I have only spoken twice. Once was in favour of having a referendum on Maastricht and the other was supporting Caroline Cox in the debate on Nagorno Karabakh.

'My father died in 1966, but it wasn't until 1970 that I plucked up courage to take my seat and make a maiden speech. That was largely due to Lady Masham—Sue. She was made a life peer, and that happened to coincide with Alf Morris' Disabled Persons Bill, which passed through the Commons and then came to the Lords. I knew Sue quite well, and I knew she was going to take part in the debate. So I felt I couldn't hover about on the touchline any longer!

'We started to have meetings about the Bill to try and put forward amendments to make it better. That's what really started me off. We, the four of us in wheelchairs, were known as the Mobile Bench: Sue Masham, Davina Darcy de Knayth, Mike Crawshaw and me.

'There wasn't really a prayer group of any kind in the House of Lords at that time, but then David Stileman arrived as Yeoman Usher of the Black Rod, and he is a strong believer. He and I used to meet in his room for about five minutes once a week just to share a scripture reading and have a prayer.

'Then David Watson and one or two others joined us. He had a year in London before he got seriously ill, and he used to come whenever he could. Anthony Cordle came as well, and Susan, and then the Stilemans invited us to their little flat which was much nicer. Before that we had met in a tiny interview room: then in their flat we had cups of tea and lovely fruit cake!

'They were good times, and we used to listen to David Watson's tapes. We were never very many, but the members who did come valued it very much. We kept going for a long time but then all of a sudden David Stileman and I were both removed. His term of office came to an end. I was removed because Susan had a stroke and I wanted to be with her as much as I could. She went down to a rehabilitation centre and I went to live there too, to be as much help as I could.'

I asked Martin what form his own daily devotions took. 'Very good question!' he said. 'I *should* be getting up at 5 o'clock in the morning, because Susan usually wakes up at 6 and if I don't get a quiet time in before that then it's difficult afterwards. I'm afraid I very, very often don't manage that. But when I do manage it I have half an hour's quiet time between 5.30 and 6. I try to get into one of the Bible stories and imagine, for instance, that I am in the upper room. I find that very helpful indeed. If I'm tired from the night before and can't get up then, I just wait till Susan is busy doing something else—painting, perhaps—and I get my quiet time in then.'

'Do you have any sense of the presence of God with you?' I asked. 'I don't mean dramatically, but a sense of the presence within you.'

'Yes,' said Martin, and as he spoke he picked up the candle that was on the table between us. 'I find this little candle a great help. When I get up in the morning I light the candle, because the marvellous light and warmth that it gives reminds me of Christ—of Christ the light of the world, and the warmth that he gives, and the fact that he can transform our lives.'

The Lord is my light and my salvation;
whom shall I fear?
The Lord is the stronghold of my life;
of whom shall I be afraid?...
One thing I asked of the Lord, that will I seek after;
to live in the house of the Lord all the days of my life,
to behold the beauty of the Lord, and to inquire in his temple.
For he will hide me in his shelter in the day of trouble;
he will conceal me under the cover of his tent;
he will set me high on a rock...
Hear, O Lord, when I cry aloud,
be gracious to me and answer me!
'Come,' my heart says, 'seek his face!'
Your face, Lord, do I seek. Do not hide your face from me...
I believe that I shall see the goodness of the Lord
in the land of the living.
Wait for the Lord; be strong, and let your heart take courage;
wait for the Lord!

Psalm 27:1, 4–5, 7–9, 13–14 (NRSV)

Anthea's story

Anthea and Christopher met when he was thirteen and she was eleven, and they loved each other right from the beginning. Both of them had a very strong call to God. It was central to their lives, and they recognized it in one another.

They were married in 1963, but in 1976 Christopher's health started to fail. In 1991, just after Christmas, he died. Anthea has known what it is to be greatly loved—but now she is having to discover a new sense of her own value in her life without Christopher. He was a music teacher, a church organist, and a highly thought of composer.

The progression of Christopher's illness to his death had been distressing and painful, and I asked Anthea to tell me about it.

'His health had been failing for about fifteen years,' she told me, 'and during that time he saw many consultants and physicians. They gave him all sorts of tests for cancer and everything else you could think of, and towards the end of the last year the general opinion seemed to be that he had anorexia and that it was a mental condition. He was very gradually losing weight, and he had a painful throat, which made his diet difficult.'

But Christopher didn't want to seek psychiatric help and Anthea didn't force him to do so. 'He was happy in what he was doing,' she said, 'and he was a very positive person. When he died of flu he only weighed five stone, so it wasn't surprising that he couldn't survive it. But just before he died a brilliant physician had suddenly thought of a rare blood condition that he might be suffering from, and he was tested for it the day before he died. He had been rushed into hospital with this bad bout of flu three days after Christmas. He had played for all the Christmas services, and two days after that he had collapsed and passed out.

'I got him to hospital in an ambulance and they revived him. They admitted him to a ward, and although they had planned to take the blood test after Christmas they took it then. The next morning he died. But they still sent the blood test to St Thomas' Hospital. Four weeks later it came back, and the physician's diagnosis had been right. He had a condition called hypobetalipoprotanaemia, which causes the non-absorption of fats, and it is incurable.'

I wondered if Anthea had lost any sense of her own value through losing Christopher. 'Yes,' she said. 'I've had to work through that, and I have gradually come to a better place. But many of the widows I have talked to have felt a loss—and I certainly felt it—that you are no longer your husband's wife. I was no longer a composer's wife. He spent quite a bit of time going up on the platform and being applauded—and we would go round together and do things together. So we weren't doing that any longer and that was a gap.

'I had been meeting people as the composer's wife, but I've realized that I've got to build up my own life. I don't do sculpture, but I imagine chipping away at a block and forging my own identity. I'm sure I wouldn't have done this if I hadn't been widowed, so perhaps that's a blessing—being forced into a position of having to do it.'

I understood what Anthea meant. 'Yes,' I said, 'because I suppose that from the age of eleven your life has been a life in union with another person . . . a human person.'

Anthea thought back to what it was like then. 'All through our lives,' she said, 'there were many occasions when I actually suggested texts which Christopher used for his music. I think perhaps one of the things which attracted him to me was my love of literature. So that's one of the things that I don't do any more.'

I wondered how she was getting on with building her own identity. 'Slowly,' she said. 'But it is happening. This retreat has been very restorative, creative: finding what's deep inside me. Giving me confidence. I think one of my great failings is lack of confidence. I don't know why, but it has always been my problem.'

I asked her what it was that she lacked confidence in, and what things were helping to give her more confidence. 'I lack confidence in my abilities, I suppose,' she said 'and for the last few years I haven't had time to do anything but look after a very disabled sick mother. She has died now, but there has been a sort of frustration and anger inside me for the last few years at not being able to get on and do this building business. God obviously wanted me to look after my mother—and my son hasn't been very well, and when my father-in-law died I was the only relation in the country who could be with him and sit with him as he died. But for a lot of the time I felt very frustrated, because I wanted to get on with the business of building up a new life, and I felt that somehow I was being stopped.'

'When I get home', I said, 'I'll send you a copy of *Leaf by Niggle*. It's actually by Tolkien, and it's the story of Niggle who wants to paint a tree but keeps getting interrupted by his neighbour. I won't tell you the story, but when Niggle gets to the other side the interruptions from the neighbour are some of the most glorious bits in the painting. It's the most wonderful story and it always reduces me to tears—and I think what Tolkien is saying is quite important in terms of how growing and building really happen.'

I asked Anthea what was building her up at the moment in terms of her Christian faith. 'It's the encouragement of other Christians and the example of other Christians—like Joyce Huggett and David.

It's very infectious. I don't know many people who have that quality about them—non-judgmental, and with a broad encompassing of all the denominations, and seeing the best in all of them.'

A few hours after we had finished talking Anthea said she wanted to add a postscript to our interview.

'Before my mother died last October I had an operation for the removal of some polyps in my colon, and when they sent them away for analysis one of them appeared to be in the very early stages of malignancy. The surgeon will have to look at me every six months now, and probably for the rest of my life, but he says that there shouldn't be a problem so long as he keeps an eye on everything.

'I found it a little scary, but having come through the other side I feel very strengthened and cherished by the medical profession. I was given a private room, and I suddenly find that I had all sorts of friends I didn't know I had.'

'What did it feel like to think that you might have cancer?' I asked. 'Well, even now I'm paying attention to my diet,' she said, 'but perhaps because I had already lost my husband I wasn't so scared. I can't put it into words, but I'm not afraid of dying and I'm not afraid of being dead. Perhaps I'm just a little bit scared of things that could happen in the process. And it's a bit lonely when you don't have your own husband to visit you.'

'How dead do you think dead is?' I asked. 'Not at all dead!' she said, smiling. 'Not after the dream I had about my husband. In his lifetime he used to wear rather dull jerseys and ordinary plain colours. But a month after he died I dreamt he was coming towards me in a lovely, unknown landscape, in a sweater of millions of different, bright, radiant colours. He was beaming all over his face, and he said to me, "It's all right! Everything's all right."'

The Lord is my shepherd, I shall not be in want.
He makes me lie down in green pastures,
he leads me beside quiet waters, he restores my soul.
He guides me in paths of righteousness for his name's sake.
Even though I walk through the valley of the shadow of death,

I will fear no evil, for you are with me;
your rod and your staff, they comfort me.

You prepare a table before me in the presence of my enemies.
You anoint my head with oil; my cup overflows.
Surely goodness and love will follow me
all the days of my life,
and I will dwell in the house of the Lord for ever.

Psalm 23

Right at the heart of the Bible there is a love story—the Song of Songs, a conversation between two lovers, bride and bridegroom. Human love can show us something of the love of God, and Christians have seen the Song as an allegory of the love of Christ for the Church. The book of Revelation talks about heaven as 'the marriage supper of the Lamb'—and we can read the Song of Songs and know that God is speaking to us through the words of it.

You have stolen my heart, my sister, my bride;
you have stolen my heart with a glance of your eyes,
with one jewel of your necklace.
How delightful is your love, my sister, my bride!
How much more pleasing is your love than wine,
and the fragrance of your perfume than any spice!
Your lips drop sweetness as the honeycomb, my bride;
honey and milk are under your tongue.
The fragrance of your garments is like that of Lebanon.
You are a garden locked up, my sister, my bride;
you are a spring enclosed, a sealed fountain.
Your plants are an orchard of pomegranates
with choice fruits,
with henna and nard, nard and saffron,
calamus and cinnamon,
with every kind of incense tree,
with myrrh and aloes and all the finest spices.
You are a garden fountain,

a well of flowing water streaming down from Lebanon.
Awake, north wind, and come, south wind!
Blow on my garden, that its fragrance may spread abroad.
Let my love come into his garden and taste its choice fruits.

Song of Solomon 4:9–16

Owen Upton's story

Feeling insecure and unsure of yourself is a condition that afflicts people from every walk of life. Rich people and poor people, very clever people and less clever people—they can all suffer from it. And many of them do. I know, because they have told me so.

But if you come from the upper middle or the top end of society then other people tend to be much less sympathetic to your problems. 'Poor little rich girl' they will say—or 'Poor little rich boy'—but they won't really mean it.

When I did a diocesan job in Southwark I was aware that many of the people who worked for the Church in the inner city had a low opinion of what they referred to disparagingly as 'the white highlands'—which is where I live. But people who are middle and upper class don't suffer less because of the particular social strata they come from—and each one of us is just as precious and valuable to God as someone who lives in the inner city. Every human being is worth more than the whole world—and our value is priceless and infinite.

Owen Upton went to the grammar school in Reigate—and for a long time he had a very low sense of his own worth. He is up at Oxford doing a degree in geography now. He plays the keyboards at his church and he also plays them on the *Value Me* cassette. I asked him about his own sense of value.

'For quite a few weeks now,' he said, 'I've been asking myself if I really have got any sense of value, and what has just been brought home to me is that I am completely insecure. Not only insecure in God but in people as well.

'I've had a very difficult year in which it's been mental turmoil all the way. I've been getting tangled up in pseudo-intellectual questioning and getting confused, and I'm absolutely certain that it's all rooted in insecurity.'

I wondered how Owen's insecurity showed itself. 'It was a deep mistrust of people that was almost dislike,' he admitted. 'I think rivalry had something to do with it, and also being afraid of them. I felt that I had to impress them, which is quite bizarre, because I have never advocated that as a way of getting along. If I was telling someone how to live I would never stress that they had to impress people. That's come up from somewhere in my subconscious.'

'But that's what people want to hear—how it is for you,' I told him, 'and they're interested to know how it feels for you. So if you had been managing to impress people yourself, would that have made you feel good?' Owen thought for a moment.

'No,' he said, 'I don't think so. I have a very good group of friends at Oxford. And I have a very good group of friends in Reigate who are all Christians. I just feel complete in their presence. I don't have to worry about who I am or what they feel about me. I know we have got something that a lot of people don't have—and I'm very fortunate to have it. But it has caused problems as well, because I haven't grown up as quickly as I should have done.'

'Why not?' I asked. 'Because I think my life was slightly sheltered,' he said. It sounds as if I'm slagging the group off, and I'm not. I wouldn't ever do that because I'm still quite dependent on them. It's great fellowship and I value it enormously. They're very close friends. We've stuck together and grown as Christians, and we all feel that God has put us together for a purpose and that he's going to use us in the future. That's nice. But I think that, on the whole, Reigate is quite a sheltered environment, and when you get out of it you discover things about yourself that you don't like and that you have to change.

'School was mixed for me. I enjoyed a lot of things about it, and I wasn't bullied. But I think I was regarded as somewhat strange by quite a lot of people, and, because I wasn't very physical or very strong, I wasn't confident about defending myself. I never have been. Fortunately I've never had to try, but that worry has always been there and it's still a worry. I think people treated me with caution because I did quite well academically. I suppose I was quite good, and I did well until I was in the sixth form. Then I did all right but not spectacularly well.

'There was an awful lot of competition at the grammar school, and a lot of rivalry. Then I did the entrance exam for the university—and I enjoyed it. I went up for interview and I thought I'd messed it up. But I got in to St John's College, which is great.'

Owen had never *felt* very loved—even though he knew that he was loved. Somehow the head knowledge hadn't quite got to his heart. But one day God showed his love for him in a special way that really did reach deep down inside him. He told me how it happened.

'In my first year at Oxford I got the gift of tongues, and it was just like being embraced by God. When I got it I was quite overwhelmed by the Spirit. I had been praying with a friend in my room, and I was sceptical that it would happen even though we were praying that it would. Then God just hit me. It was an unforgettable experience and a real boost to my spiritual life. I knew that God was there and that I had experienced him, and it was a real beacon.'

'Do you still use your gift of tongues?' I asked. 'Yes,' he said. 'I find it very useful for expressing things that I can't express through language. Today I seem to be doing reasonably well, but a lot of the time I am hopeless at expressing myself in language and in words. I can express myself much better on paper.'

'So it's good that the words are coming today.' 'Yes, I'm surprised about it,' he said. 'But it's reassuring, because it means I can hold things together. And I'm not having to think about it, or make myself speak. I'm just naturally saying it.'

'Has your awareness of the love of God been consistent?' I asked. 'No,' he said. 'It certainly hasn't—generally because having learned quite a lot I turn my back on God and try and work things out by myself. All last year I was having an intellectual wrestle about a lot of things—and that is necessary for Christians, so that they mature in their faith. But my insecurity stopped me from reaching logical conclusions.'

I wasn't sure what the connection was between insecurity and intellectual wrestling. 'It's pride,' Owen said. 'Pride and insecurity are two sides of the same coin. We want to be in control.'

I began to understand. 'So if we were in control,' I asked, 'then we could hold our head up high for the wrong reason. Like the Frank Sinatra song . . . *I did it my way.*'

Owen nodded. 'Yes. Oxford is a big place for enquiry—scientific and philosophical—and if you are studying you will ask questions.' 'But that's good, isn't it?' I said. 'Yes, but where I fell down was asking questions on the wrong side. I was asking God questions and asking questions about God, and seeing God as small enough for me to treat him like that.

'Christian academics have said to me that I had to recognize that I wasn't very big, and that God is far greater than we are. So when we're asking questions we need to be humble, and to realize that we're not going to get all the answers. I was saying to God, "Why have you done this?" and, "Why have you done that?" . . . "I have a right to know." But I haven't really—not in a lot of cases.

'Pride is wanting to be in control and wanting to be God—and that is going to make you insecure because you aren't God and you can't be. You're going to fail every time.

'But once you know that God loves you then you start to feel differently about other people. I had been wondering why I was feeling so hard-hearted towards other people, and I really was. I still do to some extent. But I noticed that in the two great commandments Jesus said, "You shall love the Lord your God with all your heart and with all your strength and with all your mind," and then he said, "and you shall love your neighbour as yourself." I think that "as yourself" is quite important, because unless you love yourself you can't love your neighbour.

'At school I got into the habit of putting myself down a lot, and I think that was partly pride and partly insecurity.' 'Meaning that if you put yourself down first then nobody else will do it for you?' I asked. 'Yes,' he said, 'that's part of it. But there were two elements to it. I didn't have a very good opinion of myself and I didn't like myself very much.'

'Do you like yourself better now?' I asked. 'Yes,' he said, 'I think I do. Because I know God does. I don't like a lot of the things I do. But I know that God made me as I am, so there's some respect there which wasn't there before. And once you know that God loves you then you can start to love yourself.'

I wanted to know what Owen's true value was in his own eyes. He thought for a moment. 'My true value? I can't see that you can have any true value except in the eyes of God. There can't be any true value in the world. I couldn't be satisfied with a high position in society, or a well-paid job or a large house, because I know those things don't bring satisfaction. They don't make you happy. I know they aren't the answer. So ultimately the only thing that can assure me of my worth is a loving relationship with God.'

'Tell me I'm loved!' That is the title of this chapter and the request that Phil's song makes—and that is what we long to know: that we are loved. When I was a small girl I learned a song at the Baptist Sunday school that I went to just twice in my life. But I never forgot the words and then a day came when I committed my life to Christ and asked him to come into my heart:

Wide, wide as the ocean, high as the heavens above,
Deep, deep as the deepest sea, is my Saviour's love.

Most of us are just paddling on the edges of that ocean of love. We have hardly begun to realize how immense God's love is for each one of us, and how enormous our value is to him.

The person who wrote Psalm 18 knew it, though, and he knew that God didn't help him and rescue him from his distress because it was God's moral duty to do it. God did it for the most lovely and satisfying reason—because he delighted in him.

God delights in every one of us, and every one of us is of immeasurable and priceless value to him. If we don't feel that we are, then we can cry out to him in our distress and our helplessness—just as the Psalm writer did in his distress.

The cords of death entangled me;
the torrents of destruction overwhelmed me,
The cords of the grave coiled around me;
the snares of death confronted me.
In my distress I called to the Lord;
I cried to my God for help.

From his temple he heard my voice;
my cry came before him, into his ears...

He reached down from on high and took hold of me;
he drew me out of deep waters.
He rescued me from my powerful enemy,
from my foes, who were too strong for me.
They confronted me in the day of my disaster,
but the Lord was my support.
He brought me out into a spacious place;
he rescued me because he delighted in me.

Psalm 18:4–6, 16–19

*After this, Jesus went out and saw a tax collector
by the name of Levi sitting at his tax booth.
'Follow me,' Jesus said to him, and Levi got up,
left everything and followed him.*

*Then Levi held a great banquet for Jesus at his
house, and a large crowd of tax collectors and
others were eating with them. But the Pharisees
and the teachers of the law who belonged to their
sect complained to his disciples, 'Why do you eat
and drink with tax collectors and "sinners"?'*

*Jesus answered them, "It is not the healthy who
need a doctor, but the sick. I have not come to call
the righteous, but sinners to repentance.*

Luke 5:27–32

4

HE CAN UNDERSTAND THE PAIN

One of the worst pains in the world is the pain of rejection. Perhaps we love someone, and they don't return our love. Or else they stop loving us and leave us for another love. Another form of rejection is to lose our job—or not to be successful when we apply for one.

Some years ago I went to bed on Saturday night weeping bitterly—and when I woke up on Sunday morning I was still weeping. The man I had fallen in love with didn't love me, and there was no future in our relationship. So I broke it off—and broke my heart in the process. Hearts are very fragile and very break-able—and I have always recognized the truth of C.S. Lewis' words in *The Four Loves.*

> To love at all is to be vulnerable. Love anything, and your heart will certainly be wrung and possibly be broken. If you want to make sure of keeping it intact, you must give your heart to no one, not even to an animal. Wrap it carefully round with hobbies and little luxuries; avoid all entanglements; lock it up safe in the casket or coffin of your selfishness. But in that casket—safe, dark, motion-less, airless—it will change. It will not be broken; it will become unbreakable, impenetrable, irredeemable. The alternative to tragedy, or at least to the risk of tragedy, is damnation. The only place outside Heaven where you can be perfectly safe from all the dangers and perturbations of love is Hell...
>
> Christ did not teach and suffer that we might become, even in the natural loves, more careful of our own happiness. If a man is not uncalculating towards the earthly beloveds whom he has seen, he is not the more

likely to be so towards God whom he has not. We shall draw nearer to God, not by trying to avoid the sufferings inherent in all loves, but by accepting them and offering them to Him; throwing away all defensive armour. If our hearts need to be broken, and if He chooses this as the way in which they should break, so be it.

C.S. Lewis, *The Four Loves*, © 1960, HarperCollins, pages 111–12

On that Sunday morning when I woke up weeping I took myself and my tears to church—to Westminster Chapel in London, where the person taking the service and preaching was Dr Leith Samuel. In the most astonishing way, the hymns, the Bible readings and the sermon seemed as if they had been specially put together to minister to me. 'Put thou thy trust in God,' Paul Gerhardt's hymn told me, 'In duty's path go on; Walk in his strength with faith and hope, So shall thy work be done.' Other verses promised an end to my sorrow and a shining light at the end of my darkness.

Give to the wind thy fears;
Hope, and be undismayed;
God hears thy sighs and counts thy tears;
God shall lift up thy head.

Through waves and clouds and storms
His power will clear thy way:
Wait thy his time; the darkest night
Shall end in brightest day.

The other hymns were just as apt, and the sermon was almost beyond believing for someone whose heart had just been broken. It was on Isaiah 42:

Behold my servant, whom I uphold,
my chosen, in whom my soul delights;
I have put my Spirit upon him,
he will bring forth justice to the nations.

He will not cry or lift up his voice, or make it heard in the street;
a bruised reed he will not break,
and a dimly burning wick he will not quench;
he will faithfully bring forth justice.
He will not fail or be discouraged
till he has established justice in the earth.

Isaiah 42:1–4 (RSV)

The servant, who is Christ, was the one we were to look at, Leith Samuel told us, and we were to see what sort of character he had and how he treated people. We were to imagine that the bruised reed was a musical reed—a pipe. And somehow the pipe had fallen off the shelf had got broken. Perhaps it was its own fault, or perhaps someone else's fault. That didn't matter and it wasn't important. What was important was the way the servant treated it.

He didn't just throw it away because it was broken. Instead he gently picked it up in his hands, bound it up, and mended it. He had come into the world in order to do that—'The Spirit of the Lord God is upon me, because the Lord has anointed me to bring good tidings to the afflicted; he has sent me to bind up the brokenhearted...' (Isaiah 61:1, RSV). Then the servant puts the pipe he has bound up and mended to his lips and blows through it—and it plays far more sweetly and richly than it did before it was broken.

Here in the rest of this chapter are four other people who for one reason or another have suffered the pain of rejection, and each one of them is discovering something of the healing power of the love of Christ. He can understand the pain that we feel, because he was also despised and rejected by men.

Helen's story

Helen Kucharek is the other singer, with Phil, on the cassette *Value Me*. She trained at the Royal College of Music as an opera singer and won all the singing prizes. When she was there she met her husband. They were working on an opera together, and three months after they met they got engaged. Then they got married, and everything was rosy. Helen walked straight out of college into a job at the Coliseum, and she seemed to have a great career ahead of her.

Helen had been a Christian for seven years, and her husband had become a Christian after they met. But she was dissatisfied with her Christian life. 'I always felt that God wanted more from me,' she said, 'and I felt incapable of giving it. I felt a great inconsistency between what was my Christian life and my normal life, and I couldn't reconcile the two. I'm a bit wild and a bit funky from time to time, and I would just be rushing out and living, with tremendous *joie de vivre*. I couldn't reconcile that with being a submissive Christian wife, which is what I thought I ought to be.

'I completely misunderstood what that meant, and I just let him walk all over me. The "me" that he had met and liked was quite a pushy person, and very outspoken—the "me" that wore make up and dressed up. But he'd say to me, "What's that stuff on your eyes? I don't like it. Take it off." So I would. And he wouldn't like my clothes. "That's not the real you," he'd say to me. "Why are you wearing that?" So I would change it. And he'd say, "Stop being a diva! Stop it! Stop being so grand."'

Helen wasn't trying to be grand, but you can hardly be a successful opera singer if you behave like a mouse and don't have any charisma. Because she did all the things her husband wanted her to do she gradually lost her own personality. "Please will you change this plug for me?" she would say to him in a pathetic voice—when she was quite capable of changing it herself. Or she would ask him to carry her bag for her—when she had been carrying her own bag with no trouble at all for years.

'I wanted him to become confident,' she said, 'and he did. But I became a mouse.'

Helen would have stuck with her marriage, because she had made a commitment to her husband. She would have continued to be submissive and mouse-like, because that is what she believed a Christian wife was supposed to be. But deep down inside she was very unhappy, and she knew that her husband was also unhappy.

One year he went on tour without Helen—with a touring

company that they had both worked for. She had left, because her career was taking off in a big way. In December 1989 she went to Brazil to perform in two concerts, and while she was there she had a feeling that something was going terribly wrong and that something was going to happen.

A few weeks before she went to Brazil, Helen had prayed a particular prayer. 'It was in this room,' she said. 'We had only bought the house a few months previously, and there were still bare boards on the floor. I got down on my knees and I prayed: "Lord, I'm just not satisfied with my relationship with you. Bring me closer to you—whatever the cost." And the minute I said that I felt as if I'd been struck. I knew God had heard that prayer.'

Helen immediately tried to take it back. 'I'm sorry,' she said, 'I didn't mean it. Forget it!' But God didn't forget it. He never does, when we make that sort of prayer and that sort of commitment. When we do we are opening up ourselves to him so that he can work within us at a deeper and deeper level. 'We know that in all things God works for the good of those who love him'—and that means in all the circumstances of our lives and in all the things that happen to us, even when those things are agonizing and painful. It isn't that God *makes* them happen, but that when they do he works through them for our good.

When Helen came back from Brazil for Christmas she and her husband were at each other's throats the whole time. 'We just didn't get on,' she said. 'I went away to Ulster to do some concerts in Belfast, and when I came back for the New Year he told me that he needed some time to go away and think, because things weren't going well between us. I accepted that. But what he actually did was to go away with another woman.'

Two months later he told Helen that he had fallen in love with somebody else. She was shattered—and she screamed. Just one, very loud scream. It gave her a haemorrhage on her left vocal chord, and she lost her voice. Not immediately, but she realized that she had damaged something. She kept on singing—forcing her singing voice out although she could hardly speak. She was doing 'Friday Night is Music Night' for the BBC and appearing at the Coliseum in *The Mikado*.

One day she was singing in the *St Matthew Passion* at the Colston Hall in Bristol, and in the last aria her voice just stopped. 'But I was the only one who knew that,' she said. 'I kept on mouthing the words, but no sound was coming out. Yet everyone else heard it. People came up afterwards and said that the last aria in particular had been really anointed singing, and that I'd sung like an angel. And I honestly believe it was an angel that was singing. It was extraordinary, and I can't explain it.'

Helen went to various specialists in Harley Street and they told her that she would never sing again. Her husband left her, and her whole world fell apart. 'The church I was going to gave me some very dubious counselling,' she said. 'They said that divorce just wasn't an option for a Christian, and they told me to "make sure that your husband has everything he needs in his marriage so he doesn't need to look elsewhere..."'

'The most bizarre things were said to me by people who I had respected and trusted, and I felt that the Church and God and everyone had let me down. For a long time I couldn't go near a church.'

Helen had lost the two most important things in her life—her singing and her husband—and she felt completely rejected. She tried to take her own life, because she felt that there wasn't anything worth living for. 'I didn't exist as a person,' she said. 'I had allowed my whole personality to be swamped—so when that person who made all the decisions in the relationship left I wasn't capable of deciding anything.

'I didn't wash for about three weeks. I didn't clean my teeth. I went down to seven stone—and I just couldn't do anything. Then some dear friends took me to the south of France for two weeks—and because they loved me so much I began to feel a little bit better about myself. But the awful thing is that it doesn't matter how much other people tell you that you're lovely, or how much other people support you, when the one person you want to appreciate you and love you has thrown you over. That sense of rejection is just so enormous.

'I couldn't believe what people were saying to me. I thought they were lying to make me feel better, and because my trust had been so abused I had no faith in anyone. Certainly no faith in God. "Why have you done this to me?" I kept saying to him, "What have I done to deserve it?" I had forgotten that prayer I had made by that stage. I am not saying that God caused all this to happen. But I am sure that he allowed it. He knew that what was most precious to me in my heart was ultimately my relationship with him.'

One day when Helen was walking round Acton she looked in through the door of a Baptist church and found herself walking in— very reluctantly. There was a service taking place, and all the way through it she was in floods of tears. She couldn't sing, and she didn't want to communicate with anybody. But at the end the minister came up to her and said, 'Welcome to our church.'

'I jumped straight down his throat,' she said. ' "I'm divorced, you know," I told him. But he didn't look shocked. He just said, "Well, that's all right. It's lovely to have you with us." Nobody pried. Nobody asked any questions. They just accepted me as I was.

'Because I had been a singer I was used to everybody turning round and saying, "Oh, hasn't she got a lovely voice." My whole identity was wrapped up in my singing. I was "A Singer!" I had wanted to use my singing for the Lord. But I realized that my priorities were completely the wrong way round. My singing was my existence. It was my persona. I was "a singer who was a Christian".'

By this time Helen had undergone surgery on her vocal chords, but the operation had not been a success. She had gone to a new singing teacher—and one day this teacher told her that she would have to go back for more surgery. Helen could barely face the prospect, but the teacher told her the name of a specialist whom she trusted, so she went to see him. 'He looked down and saw my chords on a camera,' she said, 'and he told me that it was like a ploughed field down there. But he knew how he could put it right and he asked me if I would let him operate.'

So Helen went back into hospital and had a second operation. 'Then the restorative process began,' she said. 'I was being supported and upheld by my family and my friends, and by the people in church. I was gradually starting to sing again, very tentatively. I did a few concerts but they weren't very successful.'

The surgery had been a success, but Helen had lost her confidence and her self-worth. 'I would think, "I can't do it—I just can't." I would be shaking, and I made quite a few mistakes. Cracked notes—and I'd get out of breath.

'It is only recently that I feel the Lord has been really restoring my self-worth. I've found out who I am and I'm coming to terms with myself as a person and as a Christian. The extraordinary thing is now that the Lord has given me my voice back.'

Helen believes that this was a miraculous healing, because she was told that she would never be able to sing again. Yet now there isn't a single mark on her chords, which after two operations is quite unusual. Most singers find it hard to sing after just one operation.

'But I still can't get much work,' she said, 'not at the level I used to get it. They are afraid to use me now, because I have had surgery on my chords—and that's the big taboo. They think it was nodules, but it wasn't. You can be like Carreras and have leukaemia. But if you've had anything wrong with your chords they tend to be very wary of you.

'But I have been doing a lot more singing for the Lord and he has opened some new doors for me—and two weeks ago I did an audition for a well-known conductor and I got the job. It's quite hard though, to come down from doing two or three concerts a week to doing one a month or sometimes less. So my survival has been a big issue. I've no income, so I've really had to rely on the Lord. It's extraordinary where the money has come from. Some people have just come and put something in my hand at a time when I have really needed it.'

But what Helen needed most of all was really to know that she was loved, and that was why she wrote the song 'I need your love'.

Touching the silence between our eyes
As I look at You, I realise
My life is empty, perhaps it always was;
Just don't leave me lonely because
I need You, need Your love,
I need you, need Your love.

I feel Your promise, lying on my heart,
But there is a distance too far apart.
Reach out and touch me, then I'll know You're there;
Just don't leave me dying, show You care;
I need your love,
I need your love.

I feel so worthless, why should You care?
Reach out and touch me, show that You're there;
O Jesus, tell me, what should I do?
How can I truly reach out to You?

So, if You leave me, what shall I do?
I know I need You, Your love is true.
Don't think I want this sadness any more;
No more pretending, show what it's for.

Take away the pain within,
Set me free from my sin
Take away the pain...

Ever since people have begun to know what God is really like
they have cried out to him out of their own pain and need. The
people who wrote the Psalms cried out in words that we can make
our own, to pray through, and to encourage ourselves with.

Save me, O God, for the waters have come up to my neck.
I sink in the miry depths, where there is no foothold.
I have come into the deep waters; the floods engulf me.
I am worn out calling for help; my throat is parched.
My eyes fail, looking for my God...

But I pray to you, O Lord, in the time of your favour;
in your great love, O God, answer me with your sure salvation.
Rescue me from the mire, do not let me sink;
deliver me from those who hate me,

from the deep waters.
Do not let the flood waters engulf me
or the depths swallow me up
or the pit close its mouth over me.
Answer me, O Lord, out of the goodness of your love;
in your great mercy turn to me.
Do not hide your face from your servant;
answer me quickly, for I am in trouble.
Come near and rescue me;
redeem me because of my foes...

I am in pain and distress;
may your salvation, O God, protect me.

Psalm 69:1–3, 13–20, 29

When Helen wrote 'I need your love' she was in a lot of pain, and even now singing the song can be quite hard for her. The emotions and the feelings can all come flooding back, and she finds herself asking God, 'If you leave me, what shall I do?'

'In my less positive moments', she said, 'I can feel, "What's the point of carrying on? I've had enough of pretending. I can't put on a Christian face and pretend that I'm happy and bouncy and that everything's wonderful. The reality just isn't like that." '

I wasn't sure where Helen had got the idea that a happy face with a big smile on it was a Christian face, and she thought about it for a moment, shaking her head. 'I don't know,' she said. 'I suppose it's part of my whole misconception about what a Christian is.'

'But if we look at the face of Christ on the cross,' I suggested, 'he is in agony.' 'I know that now,' said Helen. 'But I didn't at the time. I just didn't understand. Now it's a different relationship. Two people communicating with each other and able to share their frustrations and their injuries—to share everything. It wasn't like that before. Jesus was much more remote then—even though I had accepted him into my life.'

I wondered how Helen prayed when she felt very low—or whether she prayed at all. 'Oh yes, I do,' she said. 'I cry... and I shout at him. I do that all through the frustration that I'm feeling. I get like a little child who stands there crying out, "Boo, hoo…" I really do keep the lines of communication open—but sometimes I don't give him room to say anything for a while!

'But I do listen… and I do want him to speak to me. One morning I sat down to read Haggai, and I said, "Well, please Lord speak to me through this. I really want to learn something today…" And I started to read these verses: "You wonder why you don't get anywhere… why you don't succeed… why you've got a purse with a hole in the bottom. Why? Because you are concerned about building your own house and my house is a ruin."

'I just shut the book. I wondered why he was saying that to me—and I thought maybe it was because I'd just done another audition and I was upset because I didn't seem to be getting anywhere. Then I opened it again and read on, and it said that "The glory of this house shall be greater than the glory of the former house, says the Lord." So I just had to realize that I had to trust him.

'That is something I have to remind myself of every single day, and when I wake up in the middle of the night with a panic attack. Panicking that I can't pay the mortgage. Or the telephone bill. And I think, "How am going to cope?" But the Lord is just so faithful, and somehow I am still here. And I am doing more than just coping. He is really building me up and uplifting me and encouraging me.

'But I still get my moments. I still ask the same questions that the song *Value Me* asks: "Do you still find me precious? Do you still love me?" And I'll say to him, "Now come on! Tell me. Show me." I need to be told. Because sometimes I just feel worthless. Washed up. Rejected… I still get that from time to time. But things really are changing, and now my relationship with God is on a completely different level.

'I know I can trust him absolutely. "What can man do to me?" You can take away everything. You can strip me of my husband, my self-worth. You can take away my voice. You can take away my career. You can take away my possessions. It doesn't matter now if I have to sleep on the pavement. What counts more than anything is that self-worth that I have in him—and whatever happens to me I'd still have that.'

What Helen had just said reminded me of Habakkuk, so I read it out to her.

> Though the fig-tree does not bud
> and there are no grapes on the vines,
> though the olive crop fails and the fields produce no food,
> though there are no sheep in the pen
> and no cattle in the stalls,
> yet I will rejoice in the Lord,
> I will be joyful in God my Saviour.
> The Sovereign Lord is my strength;
> he makes my feet like the feet of a deer,
> he enables me to go on the heights.
>
> Habakkuk 3:17–19

'That sounds rather like where you are,' I said to Helen, 'and it seems like a very tough journey.' She nodded. 'Yes, and I'm still on it. I've by no means arrived. When we were doing the recording of *Value Me* I experienced a lot of pain. There is so much in the songs and the Bible readings that I haven't worked through yet and that I'm still struggling with. Yes, my self-worth is there in the Lord. But whenever I get a rejection, and whenever I don't succeed at an audition, I take it so personally. I know I shouldn't but I can't help it.

'The other night I was lying in the bath and the enemy just came round—and there were all these thoughts going round and round in my mind. "You're a has-been!' You're never going to have the career you have had... You're a wash-out... Your career is a wash-out. You're no good any more. You're not going to succeed. You're not going to make money. You're not going to do any of these things." And I just have to say, "But hold on a minute! Those aren't the things that I really want anyway. What I really want is to stay close to the Lord and to do what he wants me to do. So those things really don't matter..."'

Sometimes in the struggle Helen finds herself on the heights—sometimes in the depths. One day, when she was recording *Value Me*, she just couldn't stop crying. 'I still love you,' she was saying inside herself to her ex-husband. But then she suddenly thought: 'Well, wait a minute. Do you? Do you really?' She drove home so caught up with that question that she went through a red light and got a fixed penalty.

'I couldn't get it out of my mind,' she said, 'and then I realized that I don't still love him. What I was feeling was that I still needed his appreciation and his love for me. He's remarried—and I was wanting him to turn around and say to me, "But I do still love you."

'But the Lord has given me the love that I need. I know I'm valued. I know I'm loved. I know I'm appreciated. But I have to keep on playing that tape in my mind, because the enemy is very quick to turn it over to the other side and to tell me that I'm not valued and that I'm not loved.'

Since Helen first talked to me she has had an experience of God which has given her a new freedom and a new joy—so she wanted to bring her story up to date.

She was away in Singapore as a member of the ministry team with Wellspring, and they were there to encourage worship group leaders in the Methodist Church. Every day they were talking with people about music in ministry, and about freedom in worship and freedom in the Lord. But in the middle of the week Helen reached a crisis. She felt that she couldn't honestly share an experience of freedom in worship with other people when she hadn't really known it herself.

'I hadn't experienced a real freedom,' she said, 'and I just wanted to run away. But the other members of the team realized that something was wrong, and they offered to pray with me. So I agreed—but very reluctantly.

'Then, as they prayed, something really lovely happened. I felt the joy of the Lord come into my heart—and years of negativity and depression were healed. And I started laughing. Just very gently to start with. But as they went on praying the laughter increased.

'Then, in the next few days, every time I was prayed for, the Lord just increased that laughter and that joy in my heart. In the past when I was prayed for I would always cry. But now I laugh! The Lord really has turned my heart inside out.

'So that's it! It's a new intimacy with God—and a wanting to go deeper. I'm on a roller-coaster now, and I want more. And the strange thing is that in the last two months, since returning from Singapore, a whole lot of doors have started to open up for work. Recently I had so many offers of work that I didn't know what to do with them.

'Because of what's happened,' Helen said, 'my Christian life isn't me trying to be happy on the surface. It's a happiness and a joy right down inside me.'

> When the Lord restored the fortunes of Zion,
> we were like those who dream.
> Then our mouth was filled with laughter,
> and our tongue with shouts of joy;
> then they said among the nations,
> 'The Lord has done great things for them.'
> The Lord has done great things for us; we are glad.
> Restore our fortunes, O Lord,
> like the watercourses in the Negeb!
> May those who sow in tears reap with shouts of joy!
> He that goes forth weeping, bearing the seed for sowing,
> shall come home with shouts of joy,
> bringing his sheaves with him.

Psalm 126 (RSV)

Robin's story

For nearly forty years Robin has done work that he has thoroughly enjoyed and found really fufilling. Trained as a chartered mechanical engineer, he originally worked in research and development, and twenty-eight years ago he joined a French group of companies and worked first as a project engineer and then in technical sales, marketing and business development.

One recent contract was on the Channel Tunnel. 'We were supplying five hundred doors,' he said, 'security doors to blank off

the service tunnel from the running tunnels—to let the mainten-
ance staff in to service the tunnels, and to let passengers out through
them if there is an incident. It was an £11 million contract, run from
our Paris office, and I looked after the UK end of it.'

Another development Robin was involved in was to set up a new
line of business in 'clean rooms'. An operating theatre in a hospital
needs to have closely controlled conditions for temperature, humid-
ity, and above all cleanliness—to safeguard the patients. The same
principle is used for manufacture in the micro-electronics industry,
and the manufacture of pharmaceuticals, and in other areas.

'By the end of 1993 we had got that new line of business up and
running,' Robin said, 'so there wasn't much more for me to do on it.
As well as that, the work on the Channel Tunnel came to an end—
and I only had a small ongoing responsibility for it.'

Robin's work was falling away, and when the new year came he
felt he had to talk quite bluntly about it to the managing director. 'I
told him that I didn't enjoy being underemployed, and when he
considered it he agreed that I didn't have a full-time job. We had
weathered the recession for three years reasonably well, but by
halfway through 1993 we were finding it difficult to survive. So we
had to cut down expenses on the marketing and promotion for
which I was also responsible. Because of that he wasn't able to
suggest something else that I could do. There simply wasn't the
money to look at a new business development area, or to spend on
any more marketing and promotion.'

Two weeks after that conversation Robin had agreed a release
package with his managing director—which meant that he was
made redundant. He had been aware of how things were for several
months, and he had been asking himself questions. 'The twenty-
seven years that I spent with the company had always been
interesting, because there was always something new to work at. I
travelled all through France, and it was a very challenging and
motivating job.

'But towards the end of 1993 I was asking myself, "Well, what is my
value in the company? What am I really contributing?" I kept looking
at my colleagues, who were struggling to get business, and I felt that I

wasn't fulfilling a useful role as I had over many years. I felt distressed about it, and I suppose I was grieving over my job situation.

'I think I came to terms with the more difficult aspects of redundancy in those last months of 1993. But it was still a shock on 31 January when I finally left. One thing that really hit me was the financial aspect of it. I realized that my company pension was going to be quite small—just 29 per cent of my salary.

'First of all I didn't think this was going to be enough. But then I took another look at my finances and decided that we could manage. My pension wasn't very big, but I had some income from properties that my father had left the family—four shops and my grandfather's builder's yard. The income from them has been very uncertain in the recession, and two of the shops have gone into liquidation. But I think we're going to be all right.'

I wondered if Robin's Christian faith and his relationship with God were any help to him in his current predicament? 'Yes,' he said. 'I think I may be a little unusual, but part of my Christian faith and upbringing was not to set your heart on riches and material things. I was in the Open Plymouth Brethren, and at the age of ten I had a very real experience of conversion. The experience was a feeling of quite deep sorrow for my sin, and turning away from it. It happened at a gospel service in the little church that we went to, and I remember getting into the back of the family car afterwards and crying.

'I left home when I was twenty-four and went to other churches, and I have always been very strongly taught that material things and riches would never bring ultimate satisfaction. So I have never had a great longing to amass material things. I am still subject to the normal desire to have money in order to buy things. But I believe I have been able to come to terms with the reduction in income because of the way I've been schooled for so many years—in the attitude that material things and money aren't the be-all and the end-all of life. That's part of my Christian faith experience.'

There was another area of the Christian faith that I wanted to explore with Robin. We are made in the image and likeness of the Creator God—and there is a sense in which the work that we do is a work of creation. 'Do you miss that?' I asked him, 'or have you got

'Do not be afraid; you will not suffer shame. Do not fear disgrace; you will not be humiliated. You will forget the shame of your youth and remember no more the reproach of your widowhood. For your Maker is your husband—the Lord Almighty is his name—the Holy One of Israel is your Redeemer; he is called the God of all the earth. The Lord will call you back as if you were a wife deserted and distressed in spirit—a wife who married young, only to be rejected,' says your God. For a brief moment I abandoned you, but with deep compassion I will bring you back. In a surge of anger I hid my face from you for a moment, but with everlasting kindness I will have compassion on you,' says the Lord your Redeemer.

Isaiah 54:4–8

But God demonstrates his own love for us in this: While we were still sinners, Christ died for us. Since we have now been justified by his blood, how much more shall we be saved from God's wrath through him! For if, when we were God's enemies, we were reconciled to him through the death of his Son, how much more, having been reconciled, shall we be saved through his life! Not only is this so, but we also rejoice in God through our Lord Jesus Christ, through whom we have now received reconciliation.

Romans 5:8–11

enough other things to do that satisfy you? How does the creator side of you made in the image and likeness of God function?'

Robin nodded. 'Yes,' he said, 'engineers can be as just as creative as other people, and as an engineer I've had a lot of fulfilment. But in the middle of 1993 that came to an end, and I have really been missing it. I am still saying, "What am I going to do now?" I still have to look after the properties, and I am able to spend more time looking after my mother. She is ninety years old, and we have moved her near to where we live. All that takes a fair bit of time.

'But it isn't as creative as I would like it to be. So I am in the position of waiting and seeing what might happen. I might be doing some work as a consultant for two of the French companies in the group I used to work for, and I might also administer a trade association which my old company belongs to. So by the end of April I am hoping that these things will have developed—to give me more fulfilment and creativity.'

> Then God said, 'And now we will make human beings; they will be like us and resemble us...' So God created human beings, making them to be like himself. He created them male and female, blessed them, and said, 'Have many chidren, so that your descendants will live all over the earth and bring it under their control. I am putting you in charge of the fish, the birds, and all the wild animals. I have provided all kinds of grain and all kinds of fruit for you to eat; but for all the wild animals and for all the birds I have provided grass and leafy plants for food'—and it was done. God looked at everything he had made, and he was very pleased.
>
> Genesis 1:26–31 (GNB)

Bridget's story

Bridget lived in a little cottage in Derbyshire with her husband Brian and their two dogs, Heida and Jemma. The house was set in a hollow, and a lovely footpath led on to deep steps made of flagstones. From the side of the house there was a wonderful view of the Peak District, and the garden looked its very best in the spring. Early snowdrops and winter jasmine, then a succession of daffodils and narcissi, grape hyacinths, aconites, crocuses, tulips and azaleas.

Bridget loved her garden and her cottage, and she loved her husband. She thought they had an ideal marriage, but things started to go wrong. She thought they were just going through one of those bad patches that all marriages go through, but one day when she was getting some clothes out of his bag to wash them she found a letter. She read it, and realized that Brian was in love with another woman.

'It was like a death,' she said. 'The death of my marriage. I sat on the bed for about ten minutes feeling really numb. Then I went downstairs. Brian was sitting in a chair, and I threw the washing down on the floor—and the letter.'

'Where does that come from?' she demanded. So he told her. He was in love with this other woman, and he wanted to go and live with her. Bridget poured herself out a very strong drink and then walked out of the house to a friend.

'I just couldn't bear to be near him,' she said, 'and every time I looked at him I would have totally conflicting feelings. I would feel, "I still love him—I still care for him," but then I'd feel, "He's betrayed me."'

Bridget went through a period of great bitterness. She wanted to hurt her husband, and she went to see the other woman and was very abusive to her. 'He was absolutely furious with me for doing that,' she said, 'because all his instincts were to protect her from me. I went through this whole time really wanting to hurt him. My mind was just taken over by the hurt.'

Bridget tried to persuade Brian to have counselling, but he refused. He went once, but it was a very painful session. 'He used it to make totally clear that our marriage was over,' Bridget said, 'and that there was no question of our ever getting together again, and that on no account whatsoever did he want any counselling.'

The cottage with its spring garden had to be sold, and Bridget moved out, with her two dogs. 'They were very special dogs,'

Bridget said. 'They were standard poodles, and Heida was black and Gemma was brown. Gemma was everybody's dog, and she could never believe that people didn't like her. Even my most famous dog-hating friend. Gemma just sat there looking longingly into her eyes, and she put her paw up all the time to try and make friends. I worked hard with them and they were well trained.'

But two years later both the dogs died of cancer, within three weeks of each other. 'When they had gone,' Bridget said, 'I thought, "Well, I was just so lucky to have you." And that part of my life is over now. But I have this big problem. I can't cry.

'I used to cry a lot. Brian said one of the reasons why he left me was that I cried so much. I certainly cried a lot in that last year. But now I can't cry at all.'

Bridget had lost her confidence because of all the things that had happened. But she never lost her faith. 'It stayed with me all the way through,' she said, 'and without being histrionic or melodramatic I think I really met the Lord through all this. I have always been a Christian. I used to go to church on Sundays and do all the things that most of us feel are the right things to do. And in the past I had been through a period of religious fervour. But I felt this whole awful situation put me on the line.

'I had an immense awareness of the presence of God. And somehow that counteracted a lot of what was happening. I found I was able to speak to other people much more openly about my faith. I got much more involved in church, and I did a lot more work with young children, which is really where my talents lie. So I eventually I began to live more creatively.'

I asked Bridget where her real value came from. She thought for a moment. 'I particularly need to feel valued by my friends,' she said. 'What they think of me is very important to me, and if I feel I have upset my friends, or hurt them, or displeased them, then I hurt terribly. There's still the child in me who is wanting to please my parents. I don't think at this stage that I'm going to be able to do a great deal about that.

'Sometimes I have said to myself, "The only love that is really there for you is the love of God. He's the only one who can love you as you need and desire to be loved." And I accept that more and more and I understand it a little more. It has given me immense strengh. But there is a big gap in me between what I know intellectually and what I feel.'

'How do you desire to be loved?' I asked. 'Praise is terribly important to me,' she said, 'and although I've got some lovely friends they are all fairly competitive people. So they don't hand it out too easily! But unless I get praised I find it very difficult to go on. I think my husband found that side of me quite difficult. In our early years he was very supportive. He would say, "That was a lovely meal, Bridget," or, "That's a nice thing you're wearing." I miss that immensely. And all this has taken a great deal of my confidence away.

'The things that the rest of the world recognizes—marriage, a house, my husband's status and all those sorts of things, and my dogs—are all gone. So it's no good looking to those things to feel valued.

'We had one or two lovely services in our church recently,' she said, 'and I've felt this huge love . . . God's love for all of us. Then I have come away and I've thought, "There really is some love there, and it's there for the taking." But it doesn't last. I think I have burnt myself out a bit, though, and when you're in that drained sort of state it's much more difficult to accept the flow of the Spirit.'

One of the ways that Bridget is working through her grief is by going as a volunteer to Corymeela. 'I've worked there for the last two summers,' she said. 'Corymeela is a place of reconciliation for Catholics and Protestants—mostly from Northern Ireland. But now it's international. I have worked with children . . . and with abused children, and with their families. You work side by side with them. And you see these damaged, bruised people. People who were full of prejudice and hatred. And suddenly they are working alongside people who they have never had any time for.

'The staff there are wonderful people, and I learned an awful lot. I went there to work as a volunteer, but it was the beginning of the rebuilding of my life. It was very salutary to work with those people. The husbands of some of the women were in the Maze prison for murder, and for all sorts of terrorist activities. But the women were still seeking healing from the Lord, and they were finding it. Finding that they could still be loved and cared for.

'We had a darling lady whose husband was in prison. He was dying, so they let him out into the prison hospital, and one of the volunteers from Corymeela took her every day to visit him. He died while we were there, and the love and the healing that she received was enormous.

'I used to think that the sooner they put Northern Ireland in the sea the better. But I really saw it working there—reconciliation and healing—and that's what it's all about.'

> He had no form or comeliness that we should look at him,
> and no beauty that we should desire him.
> He was despised and rejected by men;
> a man of sorrows, and acquainted with grief;
> and as one from whom men hide their faces
> he was despised, and we esteemed him not.
> Surely he has borne our griefs and carried our sorrows;
> yet we esteemed him stricken, smitten by God, and afflicted.
> But he was wounded for our transgressions,
> he was bruised for our iniquities;
> upon him was the chastisement that made us whole,
> and with his stripes we are healed.
>
> Isaiah 53:2–5 (RSV)

Kathleen's story

Kathleen had just lost her husband. But it wasn't so much the loss of her husband that troubled her, but the fact that somewhere along the way she had lost herself. All through her life she had allowed other people to tell her what to do—so she had never done what she really wanted to do or become the person she really wanted to be. I asked her to tell me how high her own sense of value was.

'At the moment it is extremely low,' she said. 'I have just been widowed, and I have never had an awfully high value of myself. I find it very difficult at the moment to cope with widowhood and with finding my real self again: the self that I would like to have been but that has been suppressed for forty years. Because of circumstances, I was never able to express myself fully, and at the moment it is very difficult.'

'What does your lack of value come from?' I asked. 'I think it comes from when I was a child,' she said, 'and from my family. In the 1920s and 1930s a girl wasn't thought of as being terribly valuable. I had one brother, and if anything was going to be done it was always going to be done by him. I used to want to do things, and I was always being told, "Oh, you can't do that..." Just because I was a girl.

'The only time I was able to be myself, and be my own person, was in between leaving school and getting married. My husband had a very strong character. He would say to me, "You do just what you like." But because of his strong character I didn't. I just did what I thought he would like. I'm not trying to put him down, but he didn't like people, and I do. So there was nobody else around. Just him and me and our daughter. I found that very difficult indeed.'

I asked Kathleen if she felt angry about what had happened in the past—angry with her husband, or angry with God? 'I used to,' she said, 'but I don't now because I've realized that the fault was as much mine as his. If I hadn't put up with it initially I think I would have become a stronger character myself. I don't blame God, because I've only just become a Christian in the last ten years. I never even thought of blaming God initially. I don't think I ever did. I thought that I had made myself what I was, and made the circumstances what they were, and I was just prepared to accept that.

'I was angry with my husband and angry with myself. And I'm even more angry with myself now when I look back and see that the mistake was as much mine as his.'

I wondered whether Kathleen saw any hope in the future of becoming her own person and of having real worth. 'I am hoping to be my own person,' she said, 'and hoping that the journey forward from now is going to be easier. Because I'm starting to accept the fact

Therefore, there is now no condemnation for those who are in Christ Jesus, because through Christ Jesus the law of the Spirit of life set me free from the law of sin and death.

Romans 8:1–2

All we like sheep have gone astray; we have turned every one to his own way; and the Lord has laid on him the iniquity of us all. He was oppressed, and he was afflicted, yet he opened not his mouth; like a lamb that is led to the slaughter, and like a sheep that before its shearers is dumb, so he opened not his mouth.

Isaiah 53:6–7 (RSV)

If we confess our sins, he is faithful and just and will forgive us our sins and purify us from all unrighteousness. If we claim we have not sinned, we make him out to be a liar and his word has no place in our live.

My dear children, I write this to you so that you will not sin. But if anybody does sin, we have one who speaks to the Father in our defence—Jesus Christ, the Righteous One. He is the atoning sacrifice for our sins, and not only for ours but also for the sins of the whole world.

1 John 1:9 — 2:2

that I can start to live with the things that I can't change. I shall change some things. I am beginning to change things now.

'I am beginning to say, "No! I don't want to do that! So I shan't do it!" Probably I shall go on much more strongly in that way, and I think that will be good for me. I think doing that is a way of reaffirming yourself. If you do things because you think other people would like you to do them that's not always good. You should do them because that's what you want to do. I don't mean that outrageously, but in the framework of life as it is.'

'Do you think you have any value in the sight of God?' I asked. 'Not very much,' she admitted, 'because I think you have got to have that value within yourself before you can realize that God values you. You have got to be something yourself first, and to accept all that you are. Until I have done that I shall not think that God values me very much. But everyone tells me that will come ...'

Jesus understands our pain. He hears our cries. He longs to restore us, to rebuild our battered lives and to give a new hope. But often he stands with arms stretched out to us—waiting for us to turn to him so that we might be healed.

We have to allow him to love us, but our fear of being vulnerable to anyone can keep him at arm's length—when he is asking us to lower the defences we have built around us, and let him hold us in his arms and love us.

Let Jesus love you

If you turn to Him, He will come.
If you turn to Him, He will come.
He will hear your cry, He will hear your cry.
He will love the child within you;
He will whisper your name;
He will take you by the arm

And teach you how to walk again.
He will lead you with cords of human kindness,
Do not fear, He will come;
Do not fear, He will come.

Let Jesus love you;
Let Him take you by the hand.
Let His arms enfold you;
Turn to Him and let Him come.

If you turn to Him, He will come.
If you turn to Him, He will come.
He will hear you cry, He will hear you cry.

He will meet you in your suffering;
He can understand the pain;
He couldn't abandon you;
He will raise your head again.
He will lift the yoke from off your neck,
Do not fear, He will come;
Do not fear, He will come.

Phil Lawson Johnston © 1994 Cloud Music

———————————

5

CHANGING ALL MY UGLINESS

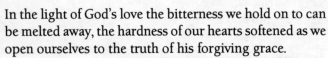

In the light of God's love the bitterness we hold on to can be melted away, the hardness of our hearts softened as we open ourselves to the truth of his forgiving grace.

The ugliness we feel in us can be the result of sin, our own or another's treatment of us, and when we look at ourselves we can see only vileness and assume that this is how others see us as well.

Our relationships can be ruined by this, and only the work of God's grace is sufficient to change us. Receiving a 'crown of beauty instead of ashes' through his love will transform our view of ourselves and how we relate to others.

O Lord, your tenderness

O Lord, Your tenderness,
melting all my bitterness;
O Lord, I receive Your love.
O Lord, Your loveliness,
changing all my ugliness;
O Lord, I receive Your love.
O Lord, I receive Your love;
O Lord, I receive Your love.

Graham Kendrick © Make Way Music/Thankyou Music 1986

'I want to help you grow as beautiful as God meant you to be when he thought of you first.'

George Macdonald wrote that in *The Marquis of Lossie*—and Macdonald was the writer who had such a profound affect on C.S.

Lewis, when on a winter evening he bought a secondhand copy of *Phantastes* at the station bookstall in Leatherhead.

As he read *Phantastes*, C.S. Lewis encountered something he had never met before, and it changed everything:

> I did not yet know (and I was long in learning) the name
> of the new quality, the bright shadow... I do now. It was
> Holiness... [and then] I saw the bright shadow coming
> out of the book into the real world and resting there,
> transforming all common things and yet itself un-
> changed. Or, more accurately, I saw the common things
> drawn into the bright shadow.

C.S. Lewis, Surprised by Joy, © 1955, HarperCollins

The God whose name is Holy is the one who transforms us and makes us beautiful, by making us like himself. One day, the New Testament says, 'we shall be like him, for we shall see him as he is' (1 John 3:2). That will be in the glory of heaven, when we see the face of Christ in what is sometimes called the beatific vision. F.W. Faber wrote about the wonder of that in his hymn 'My God, how wonderful thou art'—and the last verse imagines the glory that lies ahead for us:

> Father of Jesus, love's reward,
> What rapture will it be
> Prostrate before thy throne to lie
> And gaze and gaze on thee.

Poetry, of course. But it gets to the heart and the glory in a way that ordinary prose doesn't often manage. We are flat on our faces worshipping and adoring—and at the same time gazing and adoring. And we can do that even in this life, and that is how we are being changed and starting to become beautiful.

> Now the Lord is the Spirit, and where the Spirit of the Lord
> is, there is freedom. And we all... beholding the glory of

the Lord, are being changed into his likeness from one
degree of glory to another; for this comes from the Lord
who is the Spirit.

2 Corinthians 3:17–18 (RSV)

In this chapter there are two stories of people who are being
changed from glory to glory—and their sense of worthlessness and
ugliness is being changed as the beauty of Christ rests on them and
transforms them. They are not yet what they will be—but they are
on their way. Kim was a prostitute in Hong Kong. David was a loner
who found it almost impossible to relate to other people.

David's story

'My story goes right back to when I was a child,' he said. 'I remember
standing in the school playground, and the other kids had just spent
the break time kicking my little woolly hat round the playground.

'I remember looking through the railings in school and thinking,
"I'm different. And there's something wrong with me, because I
don't mix like the others. I'm not like the other kids. I'm a loner."
That's the first time that I realized I was different.'

When David got into junior school he would go home and sit in
the kitchen and tell his mother all about his day in school. But after a
while he began to realize that she wasn't listening, so he began to
make things up. 'I would tell her all kinds of lies,' he said, 'but she
just wasn't listening. She was like a blank wall. That confirmed for
me that I was wrong, and that there was something wrong with me. I
wasn't a person of any worth.

'I had a teacher at school who did a nice line in character
assassination. "You're not going to pass this test," he used to say
to me. "You won't pass..." He was a very pompous man, and he
shattered my self-confidence. I was often off sick, and I had
bronchitis and hay fever. In classes my eyes and my nose would
be streaming so badly that I could barely concentrate.'

When David got to the top year of junior school, things seemed to get a bit better, because he was a good reader and he could do art. 'But when I went to secondary school I hit the bottom again,' he said, 'and for the first two or three years I got bullied. People would sit behind me in class and dot the back of my neck with a felt-tipped pen, and occasionally they'd punch me on the arm or the face, or trip me up and kick me downstairs.'

David became harder and harder and started swearing at his teachers behind their backs. 'By the time I got to the third year I had an ice-cold stare,' he said, 'and I could stare my teachers out. Even my headmaster. He'd tell me off and I'd just stare straight into his eyes. And every time when I went up against him I won.'

But inside himself David was getting more and more desperate. He was lonely and he was unhappy. In the break times when it was raining he would stand in the rain outside the building and just stare into space, and he wouldn't talk to anybody.

'I found it difficult to talk to people and to have conversations,' he said. 'If I wanted to buy something I'd have to walk past the shop two or three times before going in. Then when I got in it was often a disaster, because I wouldn't be able to articulate what I wanted. It had to be a straightforward transaction. If the assistant asked me anything I was gone. I just wheeled about and went straight out of the door. I was cripplingly shy.'

One night when David was lying in bed he put his hands round his throat and started to squeeze. 'This is it,' he thought, 'I'm going.'

'I wanted to kill myself that night,' he said. 'I remember really squeezing hard, and I kept going. I didn't know how long it would take to die, and that night I really wanted to die. But someone stopped me.

'The next day at school I drop-kicked one of the bullies downstairs, and I stared the other one out. I'd never stared them out before. But this time I did. The one I'd kicked downstairs was all right, and the other one just backed off; because by that time I was ready to do any amount of physical violence to get them off.'

When David got to the fourth and fifth years he spent most of his time in the library reading books and encyclopaedias. 'Because you can get lost in a book,' he said, 'and you can get lost in an encyclopaedia. And I would just stare out of the window. I couldn't function like other people, and I was always wondering why I wasn't like other people.'

When he was fifteen he left school and went to technical college. When he was there he began to come out of himself a bit. 'We were working with steel lathes,' he said, 'and I liked that. But I started carrying a knife then: a flick-knife. I kept it really sharp and I used to practise flicking it out. I never used it. But it felt comfortable to have it there.'

He didn't do very well at technical college and he didn't get on to the ordinary national diploma course. He went into industry on a youth opportunities course and started to work with lathes again. 'I understood machinery,' he said, 'and I loved turning out bits of steel. It was one of the most rewarding times in my life.

'But sadly during that time I really got into pornography. I'd got into it first of all when I was fourteen. I'd found some at school. But now I was older I'd buy it. At seventeen I was buying it from a local sex shop. You are supposed to be eighteen, and I filled in their membership card with a false age and name and address. By then I had got pretty devious. But my parents never knew about it. Not then.'

I asked David what he meant when he said that he had got into pornography. 'Did you get photographed?' I said. 'No, I was passive, if you like. Using it.' 'Was it a turn-on for you?' I asked, and he said, 'Yes. But it was also a refuge.

'My mother had set phrases that she used towards me,' David said. 'Don't marry a local girl.' 'Get yourself out of this city.' 'You ought to do something with yourself.' That sort of thing. I can't remember the others, but they all had an immense ability to make me want to do absolutely nothing. And in three years that's what I did. Absolutely nothing.

'That was the loneliest time. Every day I'd vanish out into the countryside. Whatever the weather I'd be out on my bike and I'd cycle twenty miles in a day. I'd go all over the countryside. I know that part of England like the back of my hand. I know every footpath and every track.

'I used to hunt for pornography there. When truckdrivers have got a stack of magazines that they want to get rid of they just chuck them in a carrier bag and lob them into a layby. I knew all the places to find them, and I'd put them in all the old derelict houses that I'd go into. There's probably still some there! I must have been in every derelict house in the area.

'It was like running away, and I did that for three years. And I used to talk to myself. I'd be cycling down a country lane and talking to myself. I can't remember what I said. But once I tried giving my life to the devil. I said, 'I'm going to give my life to the devil.' Then I said, 'No, I'm not.' I meant it when I said it, but I rescinded it.

'It was weird. I was just wandering, and going to millions of places. I think it was because I really wanted to get away from home and I didn't know how. I didn't have the confidence to move out and get a room somewhere. So I had to do it that way. I'd be out from seven in the morning until it was dark. I think my mother thought I was having an affair with some married woman—which I wasn't.'

'You were having an affair with your pornography,' I suggested to David. 'Yes,' he agreed. 'I've never understood why I got so hooked, and why I wanted to find the stuff. I suppose it was like a challenge.'

The pornography was a substitute for what David was really longing for—a really satisfying relationship. But he had never known one. 'That was the second plank of my thought life,' he said. 'I had this belief that I was going to meet some wonderful girl who would redeem my whole existence, and that somehow it was all going to come right. I've never had a girlfriend, and I've never known what it is to have a close relationship. My parents weren't close and we were a very un-close family.'

After David had been at home for three years, his mother threw a prospectus of courses at him one day and told him that he ought to do something. 'So I stuck a pin in it,' he said, 'and came up with a course in marketing, advertising and public relations. It was a year's course, and after I'd been on it for three or four months I started to change. I began to get a bit more confident and to be able to articulate ideas. I got 95 per cent in marketing—and for somebody who thought he was thick that wasn't bad.'

Then David was offered a two-year course in graphic design, and he accepted. He was twenty-two, and the other people on the course were younger than him. 'I was able to relate to them,' he said, 'and I found my sense of humour again. I used to crack jokes at home but that all stopped after a while. But I was able to crack jokes with the people on the course and that made them accept me.'

David stayed at college for three years and got all his certificates—in advertising, public relations, marketing and graphic design. 'I was twenty-four by then,' he said, 'but I was still immature. And I was still into the porn, because I had Soho to mess around in. Then I wrote to my parents saying I was going to come home for a while—because I didn't have anywhere else to go and I didn't have a job.

'My mother wrote to say that I ought get myself a job and get on in life, and they sent me £200, which was a lot. They couldn't afford it, but they sent it to me. So I got myself a bed and breakfast in London for nine weeks.

'When you are under twenty-four they only pay your rent for eight weeks, so after that you have to leave. They won't pay it again for another six months, and then it will be for another eight weeks.

'The bed and breakfast was full of characters. There was a guy who drank nearly all the time and ate Chinese meals out of one saucepan. He'd empty them all in at once and eat them during the week. He must have got horrible food poisoning. There was another guy who was very nervous and who had been a runner in the City of London. We had everything from a skinhead who kicked the doors in to guys turning up with prostitutes late at night for the loan of a room. I lived in that atmosphere and I nearly ended up running the house.

'We had a woman living there who was epileptic, and her husband was blind. One night she had a fit in the bathroom and I had to kick the door down. Then she tried to chuck herself out of the window into the street and she was shouting out of the window. Her husband was saying, "It's all right, Maureen, I'm coming," and we had to get the police in. I managed to deal with all that, and I was amazed that I could.

'I wasn't a Christian then. But I did buy a little Bible. There was a little bookshop, and I focused on the one thing and I went in and bought it. I bought a King James Bible, because I bought it without looking at what was available. And I couldn't read the blessed thing. It was all Thees and Thous.'

David's eight weeks came to an end, and the landlord gave him an extra week for clearing up the back garden. But then he had to leave. 'I took all the gear that I didn't need,' he said, 'like my typewriter and other bits and pieces, and the King James Bible, and I threw them all in the river.'

Then he packed one bag and set off. 'This time I'd decided that I was going to be spectacular,' he said. 'I decided that I'd do a tourist trip round Britain and see all the sights—and then I'd go down to Cornwall and jump off the cliff.'

David decided that the first place he wanted to see was Oxford, so he set out to walk there. 'I went to Thame through a day and a night,' he said, 'and the sense of freedom was amazing. When you first go homeless you feel that you're really free. You can just suit yourself and do what you want and there's nobody to stop you. I've never known a feeling like it.

'But when I got to Amersham my feet were badly blistered. They were really painful, and I started to get pains in my stomach because I hadn't eaten anything. My head ached, and eventually I could only walk a few yards at a time. Then I'd stop, and sit on my pack—then I'd get up and walk a bit more.

'Somehow I got to Thame, and I spent some part of that evening shouting abuse across the fields. A police car was going by, and it must have had better things to do than deal with this loony in the fields shouting abuse at them in the darkness. That was when it really came home to me that I was homeless and that I was on my own. I came to Oxford on the bus, and my first night here I tried to sleep rough. I put newspapers over myself, but I forgot that you're supposed to put them inside your clothing not outside.

'I don't know how I got through that night. It was six o'clock when I first went to sleep and I only slept for an hour. Then I got up again and wandered around. Then I slept for another hour, and somehow I got through to the morning. I had £40 of dole money left, so I bought a sleeping bag which I used for the rest of my time on the streets. And I don't know why, but when you haven't got enough money you have a habit of buying stupid things, like crisps and coke, that you don't need. You need food. So most of my money started to fizzle away.

'I remember feeling very negative and very dead. But some of the time I was swearing and screaming and clenching my fists. My feet got better, because I treated them to some stuff in Boots. So I walked out to Abingdon and walked back. On the Saturday night I passed a church, and I decided that the next morning I'd go there, because I thought it would be warm. But when I got up on the Sunday morning everything in me said, "Don't go to church."

'My parents had always said to me: "Don't bring religion into the house." They would say, "You can do what you like about God and religion—but you mustn't bring it home with you."

'When I got up that Sunday morning I was just swearing my head off and I was really hacked off. I got my sleeping bag rolled up and tied it on to myself, and I started to walk to Abingdon. But just as I was going up Boars Hill, the sleeping bag totally unrolled itself. I got really angry and started swearing into the woods. I started to roll it up again, and as I was doing that I heard God's voice say: "Turn around. Go back."

'It couldn't have been me saying that, because I'd never tell myself to go back anywhere. So I rolled the bag up again and turned round. I put a bit of a spurt on to get back even though it hurt my feet. I walked back down the river and I came up into the church in time for the evening service. I sat down on a seat—and I was worried, because I'd been on the streets for two or three days. I hadn't had a bath and I was a bit of a pongy person!

'We were given a wonderful sheet with a black cross on it and a load of writing which I tried to read. But I wasn't too conscious at the time. And we kept standing up and sitting down. We got up and we sat down. Got up and sat down. Then an evangelist called Vijay Menon stood up, and he spoke about God's love. I couldn't understand a lot of what he was saying. But some of it—about life and about people—I related to immediately.

'I had no concept of God. I had never known what a god is. I had done a lot of reading—Aleister Crowley and Christian Science and Dianetics. But as I sat there listening to this guy talking about God's love, something inside me clicked. At the end of his talk he said he was going to pray a prayer—and he said: "You can pray this prayer if you want to."

'And I did pray it. But I said to myself: "This isn't going to b—— work!" I was in a bad state at the time, and I just couldn't think how it was going to work.'

But something happened to David that night, and as he walked away from the church he started to talk to God. 'I'd found someone to talk to other than myself,' he said, 'and when I went down the towpath that night I started to direct what I was saying to God.

'OK, I was still swearing. But I was swearing at him, and I'd found someone to talk to. And I started to think, "Why should God or his Son do something for me that I haven't asked him to do?" It felt so unnatural. There's this man who dies on a cross—for me, supposedly. Yet why should he do something that I hadn't asked him to do? I kept thinking about it, because I couldn't find an explanation for it.

'But that night I got hacked off again and I was really angry. I tried to flick the blade out of my safety razor to do my wrist. But I couldn't get it out, so I gave up on that. I was exhausted and I went to bed. I was sleeping under a road bridge then, at the back of the Thames river. When I woke up the next morning I started to feel different and to get positive—and things just seemed to pick up.

'I went to the library and I researched how a homeless person could sign on. I looked it up in the DSS manual, and I was familiar with that because I'd used it to help people at the bed and breakfast. After I'd researched all that it gave me the courage to go in and sign on.

'When you sign on at the DSS they ask you for your address. But if you haven't got one they can only help you financially. They can't help you to get somewhere to live. So I signed on and they gave me an emergency payment.

'But that money went fairly quickly. After three or four days I was starving—and I wouldn't have any more money until I got the next cheque. I was wandering down St Clements, and I said to God rather jokingly—laughing—"Come on! Do something! I'm starved." And I found a £10 note outside the restaurant and I picked it up. I wasn't going to walk into the restaurant and say, "Does anybody own this £10 note?"

'So I put it in my pocket and went to the fish and chip shop. I had two minced beef and onion pies and two bags of chips and it was the best meal I've ever had. I stuffed myself—and I really slept that night.

'Then I said to God: "I've got to get out of the city centre"—because the other drunks were beginning to notice me. When you are around on the streets all day you get seen. God didn't speak to me and say: "Go across Port Meadow." But that's what I did—and when I went over the canal and down the back there was an old Thames lock house.

'There was nobody living there, and it was derelict—so I moved in. I used to walk back there every night and sleep in my sleeping bag, and every morning I would walk into town again.

'I think that began my process of becoming a human being again. On Sundays I went to church morning and evening. The first week I didn't make myself known. But then various things started to happen. I found the Night Cellar, which was a hostel for people who were twenty-four years old and under. So I went to stay there.

'Then it was amazing. I didn't have a clue what a Christian was, and there was a woman sitting in the Night Cellar, and a student-type man with a big Bible—and I was sitting there ponging to high heaven, because I hadn't had a bath for three weeks.

'That woman asked me the question that needed asking: "Are you a Christian?" she said. I thought for a bit, and then I told her: "Yes. I am."

'That's where my Christian life really began—and when I next went to church I realized I needed to go up and say to someone, "I am a Christian." But I didn't know what a Christian was.

'Then a girl asked me if I'd like to join a Christian basics group. I said that I'd like to join a group because I was a Christian, and I was signed up for one. And the next week I got the housing list and worked my way down.

'You get a lot of rejections. But on the last three I prayed. I said, "Lord, give me a hand. Because I can't be on the streets to do this basics course." And when I phoned a lady in Blackbird Leys she told me to come down and see her. So I went. By that time I had been four weeks on the streets, and I went into her living room and chatted to her. I admitted that I was of "No Fixed Address", staying at the Night Cellar. But she said: "OK. I'll give you a week's trial to see how you go."

'So I moved in. And I had five baths that night. It was a marvellous night—when you haven't had a bath for four weeks. I just fell in love with a bath. I had some money that had come in at some point, so I got some towels, soap—and some Jif and a sponge to clean the bath, because the dirt that came off was unbelievable. Then I cleaned the whole bathroom—and that was weird. Because I've never done that before. At home they couldn't even get me to clean the bath. But I cleaned the bathroom up and I went to the first basics group.

'We all talked about God. They were a bit intellectual—and I wanted to ask basic questions, which I didn't. But I listened—and I contributed. I remember saying things about God that I wasn't aware of knowing. There was some intellectual guy next to me saying: "I just can't believe that God's good"—and I said: "He is good. He must be. He's looked after me."

'After that I went to the job centre and prayed over the cards—and I got a job at a hotel as a waiter. But we used to do everything. Running round making beds, ironing sheets, cleaning loos. The lot. At the end of the day I was always knackered—but it gave me financial independence.

'Then one day my mother opened one of the pornographic mailings from Europe that was addressed to me. It was hard core pornography, and the firm had my name on their list. My mother just blew her stack and my father blew his. They sent me a letter saying: "From this day forward you are no longer our son."

'That night I was sitting in church and someone was talking about the homeless. I wanted to stand up and say, "You hypocrite!" But I didn't, I just dived over the pew and left. I stayed away for about a month. I can't remember what I did on Sundays. But I carried on working. Then one night I decided to go into town and get some fish and chips, and I heard God say again, "Turn round and go back."

'So this time I did it again. I took a seat at the back so I wouldn't get noticed. But in front of me there were two guys from my basics group—and it came to that horrible moment, "the peace of the Lord". It went through my mind, "David, if you want to leave, you've got to go now. But if you want to stay you've got to share the peace with these guys—and that means you're staying for good." So I stayed—and shared the peace of the Lord.

'They were really glad to see me back—and I was happy to be back. A few weeks after that I went to see the vicar to say that I'd like to be baptized—and I got baptized in June 1989.'

Even now life isn't always easy for David. 'It's taken me a long time to come to terms with my weaknesses,' he said, 'and I still don't make friends easily. I still get hurt by things—and it's taken me five years just to have conversations with people.'

David is able to be open about himself now. 'I'm getting less defensive,' he said, 'and this is part of the healing. It's a willingness to face the past. But when I first came here I didn't really like these people. I thought they were smug and middle class. And I know why I felt like that. It was pride—and hurt—and pain. But then I got into the work of the Holy Spirit, and I think I let the Spirit in.

'When that happened I started to realize that I could worship God. I hadn't known that before. I realized you could sing songs of praise to God and that he'd touch you. I don't know how—but I just started to learn.'

One day David was in church and they started to sing a song.

Father God, I wonder
How I ever managed to exist
Without the knowledge of your parenthood.

He says it was as if God was saying to him: 'You've got a choice, David. You can sing this song really loudly, for me. Or you can sing it quietly.'

David chose to sing it loudly. 'I blasted it out at the top of my voice,' he said, 'and it made me realize that I wanted to be a Christian. There was something really good here, and I wanted to go for it.

'One thing I have discovered is to do with how God feels about me.' David was talking very slowly now, and he was finding it hard not to break down. 'Sorry,' he said, 'it's that . . . I don't think I've ever met anyone who actually loved me. I've never met anybody who had any time for me. Or who cared for me or wanted me. But God actually loves me.

'Recently I had sex with a girl, and her boyfriend came round and hit me. And I was just devastated. I thought I'd blown it. "This is it," I said to myself, "my salvation's duff . . ." I got a length of rope and made a noose and thought, "I'm going to hang myself." I remember walking around that night and a church meeting was going on. Someone was speaking, and I thought, "You don't care—I've just been punched in the face." But it was that night that I really understood that God actually loved me . . . even after what I'd done with that girl. What I'd done was wrong—and I'd known it was wrong. But God was actually going to take me. And use me. And make me something worthwhile . . .

'It's one of the few times that I've ever said that. I used to stay in church repeating it in Psalms—the ones that say that God loves me. But I very rarely say it myself, in my words—"I know God loves me . . ."

'When I went home for the funeral of my mother I found out that she died unwilling to see me. Even when she had cancer she said she would never have me back. I was staying in the vicar's house, and he said, "Why don't you phone your dad?" But I said, "No. My dad's going to thump me. He'll plaster me into the wall. He's going to be tough." But I did phone, and my dad said, "It's all forgiven. It's all in the past now. We're putting it all behind us. You're forgiven. We're family again . . ."

'A long time ago somebody had given me the parable of the prodigal son and said, "That's for you." But I'd said, "Rubbish! My family will never forgive me." But my father did forgive me—and now he's my best friend. He's done something that is so Christian and that's so in line with what God wants. And that's been a big part of my healing. My dad and I are both men who can work with our hands, and that's what we understand. And to be back with him is amazing...

'I don't know what the future holds. But I've been reading those bits in the Bible where God says: "I've prepared a future for you..." in Jeremiah. I despair at times. But I often think that God didn't make me a loner. He didn't make me unsociable. He didn't make me any of those things. They happened. But they don't have to remain for all time. They don't have to stay that way for ever.'

Kim's story

Kim was nineteen years old—divorced, with two little boys. She left them with her ex-husband and set out for the Far East. In Singapore she went to a party in one of the big hotels, and met the man who became the father of her next two children. He was Chinese, and they fell in love at first sight. But then Kim became pregnant.

'Get rid of it...' the father said to her when she told him. But Kim didn't want to. 'He got me a place to live in Penang,' she said, 'but he didn't need me any more. I asked him if he loved me and he said he didn't. He said, "I pity you because of your fate."'

Kim had twins—a boy and a girl—and after they were born she went to Hong Kong and got herself a job in a night club. 'But then I flew back to Malaysia and I kidnapped my daughter,' she said. 'I couldn't get my son. He's still in Malaysia.'

Back in Hong Kong again, Kim got a room and found someone to look after her daughter, Marika, while she went to work at night. 'She was eighteen months old,' said Kim, 'and I was in the bar scene and the nightclub scene. I hated every minute but I had no choice. There was no other way I could survive. I had no qualifications. So I did what I had to do.'

For eleven years Kim worked as a prostitute. 'I had to give my body for money,' she said, 'and I hated it. Someimes I'd pray, and I'd say to God, "I need to make money tonight." I didn't know God could hear me—but when I prayed like that I would make money, and I wouldn't have to do anything for it. People would just say, "Thank you for being such a nice person tonight in the night club, and for being a host, and for being talkative. This is a present for you." And they might give me a thousand dollars.'

Kim went on working in the night club, but she still hated it. 'You had to get drunk to hold a conversation,' she said. 'Not very drunk, but it made it a bit easier. Because it was hard to sit there showing your boobs to every Tom, Dick and Harry. It was really difficult. Sometimes my boss would call me a drunken peacock, because I strutted. But she was kind in a way, because she'd say "You look nice ... you look lovely ..." She belonged to Boxer Smoker Table Number 1 which is a charity organization, and sometimes it was our job to go out and raise money. To hassle men, rich men, to buy raffle tickets and to spend so that we could get money to give to children.

'When we did that it was wonderful. Not to have to do any bad thing that night, but to dress up really nice and then just gently ask them for money. Bankers, lawyers and judges and people like that. They had lots of money—so it wouldn't hurt them to give a couple of thousand dollars. I used to look forward to that every year.

'But on the other nights I'd have to go out with all kinds of men. I used to want to get wined and dined so that I could get to know someone over dinner. If I liked him I would go to bed with him. If I didn't I would say, "Thank you very much for a lovely evening— and goodbye and goodnight." But most of the time I did go to bed with them, because I needed the money.

'Sometimes, though, the men just wanted company, and sex wasn't what they came for. It was lovely to realize that some men aren't terrible and that some of them are really generous. It was wonderful. Because I didn't have a boyfriend or a husband or a lover I used to make do with what I could get. If I met a man I liked then I'd have him for myself that night. He still had to pay. But I'd have my cake and eat it.'

But Kim hated the job that she did—and she hated the life that she was living. One of her close friends choked to death on her own vomit. 'She was an ex-drug addict,' said Kim. 'She had been on heroin—and she had kicked that habit but then she needed a substitute. She needed alcohol—and amphetamines—to get the buzz. She was a very kind girl—and always buying people little presents. I would love to know that she's with the Lord now. I know she was a Catholic—but she wasn't a strong Catholic—and she was like a lost soul.

Two more friends of Kim died. They were prostitutes too, and they both died alone in their rooms. Kim found one of them—and she must have been dead for four days. Her cats had been shut up in the flat, and there was a terrible smell of their faeces and of the decomposing body of Kim's friend.

One day Kim rang up her mother in the USA. 'Once in a while she'd send me a birthday card,' she said, 'and I thought I must phone her. I had no idea what to talk about—because we hadn't been in touch for years. But we talked for a whole hour, and it cost me $100. And I kept on phoning her. Sometimes I'd be very drunk, and she was worried about me. I think it must have preyed on her mind, because one night she said to me, "Why don't you come to America?" I'd waited twenty years for her to say that to me—so I went, with my daughter, Marika.

'It was just wonderful to see my mother. We didn't know what to say to each other—but there was hugging and there were tears. We talked over the old times—and I still don't really know why she left me, or who my father really is.'

One day Kim's half-sister invited her to church, and she began to realize what God could do for her. 'That day was really lovely,' she said. 'There was nice folk music. And a sermon explaining to us about the Lord Jesus and who he really is. I'd always known he was the Son of God—but I didn't know that he had died for me. When I was a child I sometimes used to look at Jesus on the cross and I'd feel so sad. I'd cry—and I'd think, "How could anybody do that to him?" But I didn't know he was the saviour of the world . . .

'Then Don Duncan, the pastor of Calvary Chapel said, "We're going to be having a communion, and there are also going to be baptisms here. So if anyone wants to be born again and saved just feel free to come down. We'll be waiting..." So Marika and I just walked down and we gave our lives to Christ, and Alleluia! We're here!

'After walking out of the river it was a really strange feeling—that someone was with me, and looking after me. I started to cry. I went and had a hot shower, because it was cold that day, and I was still crying. But then I just started to worship God.

'There was a lot of healing that needed to be done, and I was for ever crying. Crying and crying and crying. At first the enemy tried to make me sleep in church and I started dozing off. But I said "No! I'm not going to sleep. I'm not. I want to listen. I'm hungry for the word of God."

'I couldn't understand all of it, even though I wanted to absorb it all. But bit by bit, and slowly, I had more understanding of it. I still had a lot of crying to do, and I had a counsellor then. She was a lovely person, and she was really good to me.'

Kim prayed that she and Marika would be able to stay in America, but it wasn't possible. So they came to England. They had been given the name of someone in London, and as soon as they arrived Kim rang him up. He hadn't known they were coming, but he found them somewhere to stay for the night.

'The next day he took us to the Foreign Missions Club in London,' said Kim. 'It's a wonderful place. He explained to the receptionist that we didn't have much money—and that's when I really started to pray.

' "Do we stay in London?" I prayed, "or do we come to Oxford?" Oxford's my home town—and every time I said "Oxford" I got the most wonderful peace inside. So we came to Oxford. I didn't know anybody and we were homeless. So I got a taxi to the police station—and they were so kind to us. They phoned up the home-less families office for us and explained our situation, and we had a bed and breakfast in the Cowley Road.

'It was horrible and dirty—and I just cried and cried. But I thought, "Well, something's got to get better." I was relying on God for all this—and he knew that.

'The room wasn't very big. Just big enough for a bed and a chest of drawers. I made one half if it into a lounge and one half into a bedroom—and I got it really nice. We were on the third floor, so I went down three lots of stairs to the kitchen to make food. Then I'd carry it up, and then I'd take the plates down again to wash it all up. But God was really with me. I know he was.'

Finally, Kim and her daughter were offered a flat, and they moved in.

'An American lady called Gerry whom I met at the Foreign Missions Club had recommended a church in Oxford. So I went straight to the parish office and said, "Hello! My name's Kim and this is my daughter Marika and we need fellowship." They put us in touch with Mary Reid, and she's fantastic. I've claimed her as my adopted mother—the mother I've never had and always needed; and her husband Allan is like a father to me. Marika treats Mary and Allan like Grandma and Grandpa.'

Inevitably, Kim had entered into the Christian life carrying a heavy load of guilt and sin. It is the same for all of us—but we don't all feel it as acutely as Kim did. Perhaps that was why Jesus was so welcomed as a friend by the publicans and 'sinners'—who were prostitutes. They were much more deeply aware of their need of his love and forgiveness than respectable people were.

At a Christian centre called Harne Hill, Kim had got rid of her guilt. 'I didn't realize that I had a lot of garbage to give over to the Lord,' she said, 'and the way they liked you to give it over was to put the cross between you and the person you were praying for. Then you could say to God, "I can give you this person now..." It's so easy. I'd say, "Lord, I put the cross between this man and me. Take care of him now—and I'd like your forgiveness for the past." That's how you get rid of it. Otherwise you are for ever carrying the sin.'

Our greatest need is for forgiveness and to forgive others. The damage that guilt can do to us is not only psychological but can even sometimes result in physical ailments.

We cannot hide. There is nothing that God doesn't see, and receiving his forgiveness unlocks and frees us from the bondage of sin that blinds us and prevents us from enjoying all the blessings that he longs to give us.

Forgiveness

How great the love that bought us freedom;
Embracing death that we might live.
When men in ignorance were killing,
You were willing to give.

The perfect Lamb given for sacrifice,
You carried all our guilt and shame.
You bore the stripes that gave us healing,
Revealing in Your name, Your...

Forgiveness, flowing free;
Your hand of grace reaching out
To meet my need of mercy.
Forgiveness flowing free
Your heart of love, pouring out to me.

Lord, You have searched me and You know me;
No hidden parts You cannot see.
Freedom comes from not concealing,
But revealing how much I need Your...

Forgiveness, flowing free;
Your hand of grace reaching out
To meet my need of mercy.
Forgiveness flowing free
Your heart of love, pouring out to me.

Forgiving others who have wronged us
Is the hardest part of all.
Our debt of love never ceases,
But increases our call for...

Forgiveness, flowing free;
Your hand of grace reaching out
To meet my need of mercy.
Forgiveness flowing free
Your heart of love, pouring out to me.

But God demonstrates his own love for us in this: While we were still sinners, Christ died for us. Since we have now been justified by his blood, how much more shall we be saved from God's wrath through him! For if, when we were God's enemies, we were reconciled to him through the death of his Son, how much more, having been reconciled, shall we be saved through his life! Not only is this so, but we also rejoice in God through our Lord Jesus Christ, through whom we have now received reconciliation.

Romans 5:8–11

6

THE CHILD NEVER KNEW

I was sitting on a bus when I saw the poster. Stuck on the bus shelter, it said that 'One in every eight people who walk past this poster was abused as a child.' Since then I have seen it in a lot of different places in different towns and cities—put there by the National Society for the Prevention of Cruelty to Children.

My bus was full of people, and there were a lot of people walking past the poster. Far more than eight. More like forty-eight. I started counting, and wondering. Which person was the one in eight who had been abused as a child? I knew that out of any forty-eight there wouldn't be exactly six who had been abused, but the NSPCC had expressed their appalling figures in a way that hit very hard.

But abuse isn't only sexual abuse. Webster's Dictionary says that to abuse is 'to attack in words . . . to put to a wrong or improper use; to use so as to injure or damage.' Here in this chapter are the stories of four people who were abused in different ways, but who are in the process of being healed.

Mel was abused sexually by her stepfather and some of the men he worked with—and it was after hearing her story that Phil wrote his song, 'The child never knew'. Margaret was also abused sexually—when she was six years old—by the boy who lived next door. The experience was so horrific that she buried it deep inside herself, and it didn't emerge again for forty years. Barbara was abused out of ignorance, because her parents had no idea how much damage it would do to send her away from home for several years— a bewildered and unhappy six-year-old, strapped to a hospital bed in a foreign country where she didn't even speak the language. Mary was abused and attacked with words.

When I was a small girl my grandmother would sometimes quote a poem that she liked—usually when someone had said something to her that she didn't like! I always remembered it, because it made me aware of the great power of the words that we say to one another.

Boys flying kites haul in their white winged birds,
You can't do that way when you're flying words.
'Careful with fire,' is good advice we know,
'Careful with words,' is ten times doubly so.
Thoughts unexpressed may sometimes fall back dead,
But God himself can't kill them once they're said.

Will Carleton

God can heal the wounds that the words have made, but the scars of the hurts will be there for always. Mary's story tells us about the terrible power that words have to inflict wounds on a child—and also about the wonderful power of Jesus Christ, who is the living Word of God, to heal those wounds and to love the child within.

Mary's story

Mary was one of three children from a broken marriage. 'I'll try to put it fairly,' she said, 'but my parents' marriage was a complete disaster from the word go. They were both very young and very immature when they got married, and Dad just wasn't adequately equipped to be a husband or a father. He had a lot of rage and a lot of anger inside him, and I think that he had a lot of psychological problems.

'I'm one of three. I have got an elder sister and a younger brother. A year after I was born Mum ran away and my sister and I were sent to a Norland nanny home. Then she came back and said she'd never leave my father again—and they had my brother. But she did do it again. She left with me and my sister and brother. Dad came home from work one day and the house was stripped.

'I never understood what was going on, but I got used to being without Dad. Mum managed to make ends meet by doing various jobs. But then she fell in love with someone. He worked out of England, so she had to make a pretty stark choice. Either she went with him or she stayed with us. She chose to get married a second time, and she took my brother with her. And I don't know if it's fair, but the way I see it is that she actually abandoned me and my sister.

The sister was sent to boarding school, but Mary was sent to live with her father. 'He had just remarried,' said Mary, 'and it was appalling. My stepmother didn't want me there and she made it absolutely plain that she didn't. She was an absolute cow, and she practised an extremely subtle form of mental cruelty on me for eight years. It was totally relentless.'

'One day my stepmother had cooked a meal, and when she gave me my plate there was a thick layer of salt all over my food. So I said, "Dad, I'm sorry, I can't eat this." She said, "Oh, darling, your daughter won't even eat my cooking"—and then he just screamed at me. "Get out! Get out! If you don't want to eat it then get out!"'

Sometimes the stepmother would burst into Mary's room in the middle of the night. She would turn the light on, and then just stand there looking at Mary.

'She always had something wrong with her,' said Mary, 'and she was a complete hypochondriac. She was always flopping around and saying she couldn't do anything, and she was a real slut. She never did any housework and she never did any ironing. I was only ten years old, and I was really confused, because I'd gone into this complete mayhem from a really well run household. My Mum was very conscientious and very houseproud.

'I think I reminded Dad in some ways of Mum. It wasn't so noticeable when I was younger, but as I got older and began to go through puberty he became very erratic. He used to scream abuse at me. "You're just like your mother. You can't do anything. You're useless. You're hopeless. Get out of my sight. You make me sick."

'But then the next moment he'd be extremely loving. "Oh, darling," he'd say, "my darling, you're so wonderful!" and he'd pay for my riding lessons and buy me things. But then something else would happen and he'd go absolutely loopy again. That was quite often sparked by my stepmother. She would allege that I had done something dreadful, but I never even knew what I was supposed to have done.

'I lived on a knife-edge for years, and I was so traumatized all the time that I was very vague, and I didn't function very well.

'That went on for eight years and then when I left home at

eighteen he cried. He just cried. I was absolutely terrified of being rejected by him. But he said the most awful things to me. Terrible things. He never hit me. It was never physical abuse.'

When Mary was eighteen she left home and started nursing. She also started eating a lot. 'I used to binge,' she said, 'and I put on an awful lot of weight. I went up to thirteen stone.' Her father worked in London, and sometimes they would meet for a meal. Mary still remembers some of the things he said to her. 'One day he asked, "What's the matter with you?" His lips curled, and he said in an awful, scornful voice, "You look as though you're pregnant." It was as though my food just turned to ashes in my mouth.

'For the next few years the name of the game was always "Keeping On The Right Side Of Dad." We all played it for all our life was worth. Once or twice he cut me off because I dared to disagree with him. He used to slag Mum off dreadfully, and I'd say to him "Dad, don't! Please don't do that. She's my Mum." But he kept doing it, so one day I sat down and wrote him a letter saying, "You know we have been torn apart all our lives. Why can't you just leave it alone?" Then he wrote a letter back to me saying, "How dare you say things like that when I've just sent you a cheque for £25." So he cut me off for nine months, and then suddenly it was "Darling, what can I do to help?"

'Then he got cancer and became very ill, and he used to play an emotional blackmail game. At one time I broke my leg, so I phoned him up and told him. "I'm perfectly all right," I said, "but I just thought you ought to know that I've had this accident and broken my leg." There was silence down the phone. Then he said, 'Well, Mary, do you realize what this is doing to my health?" So my immediate reaction was, "Back pedal! Back pedal! Because otherwise there's going to be big trouble." I remember my breathing started to go, and I started shaking and sweating. I said, "I'm all right really, Dad. I'm fine!" But it was always like that.

'As he got more ill things got even worse and then we had a frightful bust up. He was supposed to come and stay for one night, but then at the last minute he phoned and asked if he could stay for two or three nights. But we had other stuff planned, so he couldn't.

"I'm really sorry, Dad," I said, "we can't do that." And he just flipped.

'We had absolutely no contact all that summer, and that went on through the winter. I phoned him on Christmas Day, but all he said was, "Hello, what do you want." The following spring I was desperate to re-establish contact because I felt so terrified that he was cutting me off.

'I can talk about all this now because since he's died there's a great feeling of release. He's not there any more to pull the strings. It still upsets me, but before I'd be shaking and hyperventilating really badly, and crying.'

At Mary's church they prayed with her regularly, and one day she cried out to God, 'I wish he were dead!' 'Some Christians got very upset with me over that,' she said, 'and they told me I shouldn't say it. "But it's true," I said to them, "I just wish he was out of my hair." '

Because she suffered very severely from premenstrual tension, Mary went for counselling—to a psychiatrist who was also a Christian. 'She didn't bring prayer into it so much, but God was definitely there. And it very quickly emerged that one of the reasons why I am the way I am—and even apart from the PMT I'm not OK—is that I am such a driven person. I'm always trying to prove that I am worth something. My father is still there in a way, and I can still hear him saying, "You're nothing, get out of my sight, look at you."

'I know that I do too much, and I'm always trying to be better and quicker and brighter than anyone else, because I'm trying to prove something. This psychiatrist taught me that on a scale of nought to a hundred of "Where do you think you are as a good daughter?" my answer would be something like minus 200 per cent—and it would be the same for "Where do you think your father is as a good father?"

'I went on seeing this psychiatrist through the year, and that September Dad took a real downturn for the worse. I was away on a weekend with my best friend. We try and get away once a year, and there we were in Devon and the phone rang. 'Your Dad wants you," the hospital said, and they thought he was dying. So I went and it was absolutely horrendous. There he was in bed in the middle of this hospital ward, and I was looking at him and thinking, "I don't love you, and I don't respect you . . ." and he was stroking my hand and saying, "I really love you." And I just didn't know what to say.

'In fact he didn't die until the November. But when I got back from that weekend I completely went to pieces. I felt I was a piece of elastic just stretched so hard that I would never ever regain my proper shape. I felt I was going mad. I was just so strung out. It was like a nightmare: I wanted him to die and he wasn't dying. He just went on and on. It sounds really callous to say that, but I was held in this iron grip, and it was as if he was saying to me, "I've got you!" But the psychiatrist was excellent, and it was quite ironic that in the November we agreed that we had reached a good end to the counselling. Just a week later Dad died.

'I've found it helpful through counselling to realize that I am allowed to feel angry. But I shall always remember one really sad thing that Dad said to me. Two years ago Granny died, and she was our rock. She was always there for us, and we absolutely adored her. When she was dying my sister and my brother and I were with her—and it was the most wonderful experience. But I remember Dad saying, "Well, that's just typical. She goes out in clouds of glory. Ha, ha! Surrounded by loving grandchildren . . ."

'He was alone when he died. A nurse was with him, but no one from the family. I think that's tragic. I think he had an understanding of God, and I prayed so hard that he would really get to know Christ before he died. But I don't know.

'Looking back over the years it was this relentless and persistent message, "You're no good, you're useless, you're worthless, and look at you." Mum wouldn't listen to me. I had a nervous breakdown when I was seventeen and I was packed off home to Mum. But she was just so terrified of upsetting the status quo that she said to me "I am just not going to talk about it—let's go out and buy some clothes." I was never allowed to talk about it.

'I feel so enraged when I hear about children being abused, because it takes so little to destroy a child's essence. When we were at a church meeting last week somebody said that we ought to be in the business of building children, not just mending adults.'

But the child within the adult often needs to be mended, and I asked Mary if she was finding any sense of value or worth now. 'Is it starting to come at all,' I asked, 'or are you still hoping that it will?' 'Yes,' she said, 'it is happening, but it's very gradual. People used to say I was very good at my job—and I used to think that if they really knew me they'd think I was awful. And there are certain things that I have to do—like controlling my weight. Because I get very upset if I put weight on.

'I think the fact that I have done very well in my career has helped. I work in general practice and I have done a lot of further education and degrees and diplomas. But I'm suddenly beginning to think that I'd like to be at home more and spend more time with the children and with my husband. It may be that's because I don't need to prove myself quite so much.

'I keep saying to myself that I'm so blessed. I've got a wonderful family of my own—a wonderful husband, two super kids, and this lovely home. But I sometimes catch myself thinking, "What if John and the children were to die?" I think I'm almost frightened to be so happy, and to be in a good place. So all these things rear their ugly heads from time to time. But it is getting better.

'I used to feel that there was something like an animal inside me and that if I let it out I would literally roll around and bash my head on the floor. Because there was so much agony in there and I couldn't explain it. But seeing that psychiatrist has helped me to identify it. She showed me how to imagine a seething pile of mess—and then to pick out separate issues, and lay them out and look at them and talk about them. Then it becomes containable, and it's easier to pray.

'She once said to me, "You might not ever be cured. But you will be more able to cope." And I don't think that I ever shall get over what happened. Not totally. But if I do nothing else in this life I have got to give my children a happy, secure childhood, so that they grow up with confidence and a sense of worth. Then I'll be happy.'

'You will never not have been wounded,' I said to Mary. 'It's like Jesus in the resurrection. The wounds were still there—and you will never not have been wounded.'

But the wounds can be glorified—like the wounds of Jesus—although the scars will always be there. Edward Shillito's poem from the First World War cried out to God from the agony and death of the bloody trenches. He called it 'Jesus of the Scars'.

If we never sought, we seek thee now;
Thine eyes burn through the dark, our only stars;
We must have sight of thorn-pricks on thy brow,
We must have thee, O Jesus of the scars.

The heavens frighten us; they are too calm;
In all the universe we have no place.
Our wounds are hurting us; where is the balm?
Lord Jesus, by thy scars we claim thy grace.

If when the doors are shut, thou drawest near,
Only reveal those hands, that side of thine;
We know today what wounds are, have no fear,
Show us thy scars, we know the countersign.

The other gods were strong; but thou wast weak;
They rode, but thou didst stumble to a throne;
But to our wounds God's wounds alone can speak,
And not a god has wounds, but thou alone.

Mary's wounds have started to heal now, and her sense of worth is slowly starting to grow. I asked her what part Jesus and the Holy Spirit had in her healing—or if they had any part.

'Oh yes,' she said, 'it's been enormous—and I have experienced God's love in a real way. Someone had a word for me once, a prophetic word. I can't remember the reference, but it was "Be content with what you have, for God will never leave you . . ." I knew the woman was going to say something to me, and as the meeting went on she looked me right in the eye before she started speaking. I was on the floor!

'I believe God does speak like that to people through his word. I just sat there slack-jawed with the most amazing feeling—because God loves me, and he'll never leave me. My greatest fear with my father was that he didn't love me, and that he would leave me. But now God was saying to me that he loved me and that he'd never leave me. It was phenomenal.'

Recently Mary met a friend whom she used to work with and whom she hadn't seen for over ten years. They agreed to meet at the station and to spend the afternoon together. 'I was slightly nervous,' Mary said, 'because I thought perhaps we wouldn't get on. But she leant across the table and looked at me and said, "You have changed so much. Tell me about this thing of becoming a Christian. You're so calm and you look so happy. It's amazing." Then we walked along the cliff. It was a beautiful, glittering February day—and we just talked and talked and talked...'

For now that was the end of Mary's story, although it is still going on. While she was telling her story, her two small children were playing happily in the background—rooted and grounded in the security of their mother's and father's love. Mary's mother and father both failed her—but God never will. Mother love is very strong—perhaps the most self-giving love of all. But God knows that sometimes even mother love can come to an end, and through the prophet Isaiah he assures his fearful and doubting people that his own love is endless:

> Shout for joy, O heavens; rejoice, O earth;
> burst into song, O mountains!
> For the Lord comforts his people
> and will have compassion on his afflicted ones.
> But Zion said, 'The Lord has forsaken me,
> the Lord has forgotten me.'
>
> 'Can a mother forget the baby at her breast
> and have no compassion on the child she has borne?
> Though she may forget, I will not forget you!
> See, I have engraved you on the palms of my hands.'

Isaiah 49:13–16

Mel's mother and father also failed her. She let Phil tell her story in the sleeve booklet of his album *Father of Compassion*. Here is the song that he wrote—followed by Mel's story.

The child never knew what it was to be
An object of love and affection.
The child only knew what it was to be
An object of scorn and rejection;
What a tragedy! They were never free
To be what God intended.

The child never knew what it was to be
Adored and held in arms of safety.
The child only knew what it was to be
Abused and torn by hands of hatred;
What a tragedy! They were never free
To be what God intended.

Father, make up the years;
Come soak up all of the tears;
Make up for the love
That always was denied them.
Father, make up the years;
Take all the shame and the fear;
Lead them by Your hand
To wholeness and freedom.

The child never knew what it was to be
Someone of value to be respected.
The child only knew what it was to be
A captive to fear, always subjected;
What a tragedy! They could never see
It's not what God intended.

If the child only knew that nothing's hid from view;
All is seen by God in heaven.
He can restore the years and wipe away the tears
With healing love so freely given;
How He longs to see every child set free
As He intended.

'Mel never had a proper childhood. She was the illegitimate child of an alcoholic father who was sent to prison when she was five. Before long her mum was living with another man.

'Mel continues in her own words: "Fairly immediately, my stepfather started to show an unhealthy interest in me and started to try to get me alone and would ask me to do certain things. It became a bit of a habit. Mum was getting quite depressed by this time so she hit us whenever we got into trouble, or whenever we didn't do as we were told. She had a hard time trying to look after six children with very little money.

"When I was seven she married the man we were living with (P), and the situation did not improve. We children were always beaten up, either by him or Mum. Mum would make us steal from shops for her so that she wouldn't have to pay for things. She encouraged that sort of behaviour and we would be punished for not doing it. If we wanted to do what was right or good, we were told off for being stupid. Obviously there were a lot of other things; school was not really a priority in my parents' eyes, and I was encouraged to stay away as much as possible so that I could either help Mum at home or go off on trips with P, who sexually abused me a lot, as did many of the guys who worked with him.

"I hated those times, and never felt that I was accepted for myself. I always had to perform and please my stepfather and my mother by doing wrong things. I couldn't do anything that was right to please them because that always got me into trouble. I always had to do something that was bad, or satisfy their sexual desires, etc., then I would get some form of reward.

"When I was thirteen I told mum what was going on with P and she called me a liar and a slut, and wouldn't accept what I had said, and yet I had no other person to turn to. I went to see a teacher at school who, for some reason, was really special to me. She tried to encourage me to speak about it and got a social worker in, who came to see me at home but was not interested at all. Mum and P just lied through their back teeth about what was happening. They wouldn't even let him inside the house, and before I knew it he was gone and nothing was done. I so wanted to be taken away from them to a place where I would be accepted for who I was and not for the things I was made to do. Those things continued until I left home at eighteen.

"After college I left home to come to London, where I got my first job, where I was very happy in my newly-discovered freedom. Nobody controlled me and I didn't have to do what others wanted me to do just to please them. But I found I was doing it anyway. I got into drugs, drink and sex in a big way for a while.

"When I was twenty-one, after several different experiences of trying to find love and acceptance, I met a friend who introduced me to a church where I gradually became a Christian and realized that God's plan for me was different. He didn't want me to go through the hell of being abused or abusing myself with other people any more. He wanted me to have a pure and holy relationship with him. He loved and accepted me for who I was, and the plan for my life was so completely different from the one that I had built up in my own mind and that my parents had 'ordained'. It was like God was saying that it was OK; that I was OK, and that he would see everything was OK.

"As I became more and more aware of him and how he felt about me I began to open up to someone about my past; how I was affected by it. I began to realize that I was completely screwed up and couldn't relate to anybody on a normal level. I wouldn't let anybody touch me because it made me feel dirty inside, whether it was purely a hand on the shoulder or anything more. I started to go through a lot of ministry and counselling. Each counselling session, each church event or Christian conference I went to, seemed to have me in floods of tears, or filled with so much anger. I knew, as he had promised, God would never leave me or forsake me, and I was trying to trust him for that, when everything around me seemed to be falling apart. For a long time I struggled and struggled, but God was faithful, and he has shown me the way forward time and time again.

"Until we see the love of God we are bound to a pattern of life by the way that our parents have treated us throughout our lives. I was bound by that pattern until I broke free and Jesus saved me and said that I didn't have to live like that any more. I could live my life as he had intended.

"I have now been a Christian for seven years, and as I look back I thank God for the experiences that I had as a child, even though they are really painful and I still have to work through many of them. I know that God is faithful, and that he will never leave me; his plan for my life is perfect; he is carrying me and he's promised always to carry me. That's what keeps me going. That's what makes me realize that God loves me for who I am, not what I can do for him. He loves me as the person that he created."'

That is the end of Mel's story as she told it for Phil's song album. But life is still a struggle for her. She has good times and bad times, because the wounds are still there and all of them aren't healed yet. Sometimes healings can be instantaneous. Far more often they take place slowly, like the sure but gradual healing of a physical wound, or the knitting together of a broken bone. Christ heals us as we rest in the warmth and the light of his presence and his love—but sometimes it will take a person half a lifetime to be aware of that love and how enormous it is.

Margaret's story

Margaret Collingwood didn't feel loved until she was forty-six years old—because she didn't feel good enough to receive love. That was because of what had happened to her when she was six years old.

Margaret works as a freelance in broadcasting. She is married to Jeremy, who is a vicar, and they have three daughters. She told me of an extraordinary incident which had taken place just a few years earlier and brought about a dramatic change in her life.

'I always used to build in failure,' she said, 'so that I couldn't succeed. I would opt out, and I wouldn't apply for jobs because I would think that I wouldn't get them. And in any relationship I had I would always be the first to end it. I had a very negative attitude about myself.

'Then when I was forty-six this most liberating and tremendously healing thing happened—although it didn't seem like it at the time. There was a parishioner who just came too many times and he seemed to be in my space. One day he came once too often. He rang the bell yet again—and I just tensed all over and screamed and stamped my foot. As a grown woman of forty-six and the mother of three and a vicar's wife!

'Jeremy said to me, "Maggie, sit down. There's something going on. Let's talk about it . . ." And I heard with my ears what was coming out of my mouth as if it was somebody else talking. I was as surprised as Jeremy to hear what it was.

'I was telling him about what had happened to me in the summer when I was a little girl of six. Something that I had buried was suddenly surfacing and it had been started off by this person coming into my family space.

'In that summer of 1945 we had a telegram confirming that my father had been killed. We had had one in 1942 to say that he was 'Missing, presumed killed'. But now they had confirmed it, and immediately our family was in tremendous turmoil.

'While that was happening the young lad from next door who was in the navy took me off down behind the hedge and abused me. I hadn't got the faintest idea what was going on except that it hurt and I cried. Afterwards I can remember him wiping my tears with his handkerchief that was bloody. He was gentle and trying to be kind. I was distraught.

'I knew that something was desperately not right. But older people instil tremendous fear into children—and he said I must never tell anyone what had gone on. I remember going back into the house and I'd got blood in my pants. My mother said to me, "Where did this blood come from?" and I lied. I said that I'd fallen on my brother's bar on his bike. But I never, never lied. We didn't in our family. So on top of what had happened there was the tremendous shame of lying to my mother. I was coping with the terrifying pain and with my mother's unhappiness. Then in September I went off to boarding school.'

It was too much for the little six-year-old girl to cope with, and Margaret thinks that is why the whole incident got buried for all those years. She didn't remember it consciously, but the abuse and its consquences had damaged her very deeply. 'You felt that you were shameful,' she said, 'although you didn't know why. You felt that you had done wrong, and that it was your fault. That you had no right to be there. No right to be anywhere. You had to earn your passage.'

But to see how Margaret behaved at school you would never have known what she was feeling. 'I was the survivor,' she told me, 'I was the one who did the mimicking. So there was this extraordinary conflict going on of acting and bravado on the outside to cover up the whimpering fear that was eating away inside me. And it made a difference not to have a father—a strong father figure.'

The boarding school itself acted as a sort of repression, and at home Margaret felt that her family were becoming the poor relations. 'We had to live with my grandfather,' she said, 'and he didn't particularly want us but we were slightly better than evacuees. After the war ended, we stayed on as there was nowhere else to go.

'But at the same time I had this incredibly close relationship with God. I'd always had it. I knew that my mother had always prayed, and God was always part of the furniture and fittings. And I would lie in bed in the dormitory and talk to God as if he was Dad—and I didn't know which was God and which was Daddy, who I'd never known anyway. So I had this very personal relationship with this person who cared deeply about me—but at the same time I wasn't feeling loved because I didn't feel good enough to receive love.

'I had always had this great feeling about God caring for the widows and the fatherless. And I'd felt an extraordinary specialness. But because of feeling so unworthy I had locked that out.'

One day after all this had come out Margaret interviewed Jackie Pullinger—the woman who has done that astonishing work in

Hong Kong, so that through Christ and the power of the Holy Spirit drug addicts have become Christians and been set free from their addiction.

'After we had finished the interview,' said Margaret, 'I told Jackie that I would like to be able to speak or to pray in tongues. So she put her hand on my head and said, "Open your mouth and get going!" She said that it is often more difficult for articulate people to speak in tongues, and she suggested that I should do it to music in the car. So the car became a very special place for praying in.

'I cried from my stomach for three days afer receiving the gift of tongues. I cried and cried and cried. My mother had just given me some of my father's letters, and I read in them about him cuddling me, and that I mattered to him. I actually felt like a baby who was being loved and cuddled—and the fascinating thing was that whatever was stopping the love of God getting through to me went away. Something had been saying, "God couldn't possibly love you—you're not good enough—you're a sham..." All those things that I'd had to keep down and repressed started to go away—and the feeling that if people really knew me then they wouldn't like me.

'I actually felt loved. I remember feeling the warmth of love for the baby who was me, and the enormous warmth of God's love for me now. Then when Jeremy said he loved me I could actually believe it, and it was wonderful. I view myself so differently now—and after all that happened I found myself getting offered all sorts of jobs on TV and in broadcasting.'

The way we view ourselves has a powerful effect on the way that other people view us—and the fact that Margaret saw herself differently could have had something to do with the fact that she started to be offered more and more work. If we feel worthless it shows—and without our having to do a thing other people take us at our own valuation. It shows in our body language, and it shows in our face.

It also shows if we feel valuable—and we cannot appreciate our own value and our own preciousness without it spilling over into an appreciation of other people's value and preciousness. We shall—

in the right way—love ourself, and then (and only then) we shall love our neighbour and all the people whom we know.

I used to think that something Jesus said didn't seem fair—although I realized I probably didn't understand. Now I am beginning to understand. What seemed unfair was that 'to those who have will more be given and they will have an abundance, but from those who have nothing, even what they have will be taken away' (Matthew 13:12, NRSV).

Jesus was talking about the secrets of the kingdom of heaven—and once the light of the knowledge of the glory of God in the face of Jesus Christ has dawned in our hearts then it goes on shining more and more, and we know more and more of God and of the love of God.

We know God more and more—and to know God is to have eternal life. That is what eternal life is. Not just the everlasting life that will continue beyond the grave in heaven—but the relationship of love with our creator and redeemer that we know and experience in the here and now. 'I came that they might have life, and have it abundantly,' Jesus said (John 10:10)—and that quality of life shows. It shines out of us like light, and people notice. We know that we are worth something—that we aren't worthless. We know that we are loved and we know that we are precious.

Barbara's story

As a child Barbara was very much loved, but the strange circumstances of her life did not let her feel it. So she has an emotional legacy of being unknown and unwanted and unloved. Her parents had been missionaries in China, and that is where Barbara and her twin sister had been born. Her parents had several children, but not all of them lived.

'They had a son,' Barbara told me, 'then two years later another son. Three years after that the second son died, and two years after that the first son died. Two years after that my brother was born, and two years after that my sister and I were born. Our mother couldn't look after us herself because she had puerperal fever (a fever that can follow childbirth), so for six months we were looked after by the other missionary wives and nurses on the compound.'

The twins were fed by a Chinese wet-nurse, who had a baby of the same age. That child died of tuberculosis, which might have been how Barbara was infected. But if that is so then for several years it was dormant. She was diagnosed as having a TB hip when she had just started school at the age of five and a half. In those days TB was the number one killer of children, and she went for two months to a children's hospital in Manchester.

'We had come back from China,' said Barbara, 'because mother wasn't fit for China, so my father, a Baptist minister, had to resign, and he got a church near Manchester.

'I think one reason why they put me into hospital for those two months was to make me get used to being away from home. Because then I was sent out to the Rollier Clinic in Switzerland, which was a famous international centre for the treatment of orthopaedic tuberculosis—bovine TB. I went to a children's clinic in Leysin.

'My mother's dearest friend was a woman doctor who attended our birth and probably saved our lives, and she made herself responsible financially for sending me out for treatment. She and her father (who was also a doctor) took me out there, since in those days they advised parents not to come out with their children because they got too upset.

'So I left my mother at Dover and was taken across by boat and train. Dr Marjorie left me there, and I was immediately strapped on to a bed on sand bags with a sort of gutter for my right leg and a weight at the end. I couldn't speak the language, and all the people around me were total and complete stangers.

'I know that as a fact, but I don't remember my feelings. I remember that there was one other person who could speak English and she was a child. But she didn't like another English child coming along. She was jealous. So she used to translate for me, but she would translate wrongly so that I did the wrong thing and got into trouble.

'That was how things were when I went there, and it has left an emotional legacy. A sense of being unknown and unwanted and unloved. I was sent all that way away from my own home into that odd situation for a reason that I didn't understand. And I was ill and to a certain extent in pain.

'Then I contracted scarlet fever, and I was placed in a room by myself right at the top of the chalet. Everybody had to put on white coats, and everything that went in and out of the room had to go through a bowl of disinfectant—including my letters. While I was ill the tuberculosis made rapid progress and I wasn't getting better. When I went out originally the hope was that I would only stay there for six monhs. But I actually stayed for three and a half years.'

'Did anybody come and see you in that time?' I asked Barbara. 'Well, yes,' she said, rather uncertainly. 'I had been out there a year and I heard a voice which I recognized from the past. I twisted round to see who had come into the ward and it was my mother. She stayed in a hotel for a week and visited me every day for about an hour or two. But she was extremely unhappy. She hated going all that way by herself and not being able to speak the language. And she got intense migraines, so on some of those days she wasn't fit to come and see me.

'My mother came the first year, and the second year my father came and did the same thing. He visited me every day. There was one absolutely memorable day when I asked him if he could take me out for a sleigh ride. It must have been the early spring, and the whole place was covered with snow, and there were long icicles hanging down from the roofs. He said he couldn't afford it, but somehow he managed it. I was taken on a stretcher and put across the back of the carriage of the sleigh, and he was sitting beside me. I could see the back of the horse trotting along in front—and it was wonderful and unforgettable.

'In the third year my mother came again for a week, and Dr Marjorie herself came once when she was on holiday. But other than that I had only letters and they sent me photographs of Margaret and Rob, my brother and sister. I remember that I put them on the wall at the head of my bed and they curled up in the sun.

'Then during that time I had what they call cold abscesses, that came out right the way down my thigh from the TB. They burst, and I have still got the deep scars. The abscesses arose from the site of the disease and spread out, and I had a doctor who came to draw the pus off with a long syringe—and every time she did it she used to give me little bundles of chocolates.'

'Did it hurt?' I asked. 'One doesn't remember pain,' Barbara answered. 'I do,' I said, remembering my screams of fury and pain at three years old when an incompetent doctor had syringed my ear too violently. But when pain is continual and very awful (whether it is physical or emotional) it must be that people bury it, because the agony of remembering it is too great.

'Anyway,' said Barbara, 'the TB more or less cleared up, but I wasn't entirely fit. I was better, but I was by no means cured, and by that time I was ten. My parents felt that I was growing up without the family, and that I didn't belong, and that they shouldn't leave me out there. So they got me back and they both came out to fetch me.

'The family moved down to Deal in Kent, and Rob went to Dover County Grammar School and Margaret went to Dover County High School for Girls. But I wasn't cured and wasn't fit for school. I had a relapse, and I went into a children's hospital in Broadstairs. I was there for eight months and came home for two months. Then I had another relapse and went back to hospital for nearly three years. At least it wasn't far from home, and although Rob and Margaret weren't allowed to come and see me my mother came once a week and my father came once a month.

Then I came under the attention of a brilliant orthopaedic surgeon called Mr Robert Milne and he decided to operate. The tuberculosis was quiescent, so he admitted me to hospital and operated on my hip. He fixed it permanently so that I would no longer have a hip joint. Not ever. Because in those days the only way to treat TB was totally to immobilize the site of the disease. So he permanently fixed my right hip and I was told that I would never be able to sit down. But I managed to—in a one-sided way—and gradually I became able to walk more or less normally.'

'Was everyone happy to have you home again?' I asked. 'Were your brother and sister pleased to see you?' 'No!' said Barbara emphatically. 'I think they wanted to be, but they couldn't be. What happened was that everybody thought it was all over. There would be no further problems, so the best thing to do was to forget about it. From now on all was going to be well. My mother over-protected me, and so did my father to a certain extent, but he was one of those who wanted to forget all about it and behave as if it had never happened. My brother and sister were intensely jealous of me because they thought I had received, and was receiving, more attention than either of them had, although I hadn't even been there.

'I remember the day I came home from Switzerland. I was standing in the kitchen of this old house that we had, and my sister came running up the back steps from school and she threw open the door and saw me standing there. She just looked at me. Neither of us had the least idea what to say to each other. Then mother came into the kitchen and saw us—and she said "Well, I think you had better start speaking to each other, you two ..."

'Only a few weeks ago I was talking to a man whom we have all kept in touch with for years. He knew us in those days, and I said to him, "You know, Bernard, I was awfully lonely at that time." And he said something like, "Well, yes, I suppose you would have been. But you see if you come across somebody who is handicapped and not—can I say—sort of not normal, you don't know what to do and what to say. So you just forget they're there because they're different." He put into words exactly what everybody was doing. They hadn't known me, so they couldn't accept me.

'I gave a party a few years ago, and something rather strange happened. Rob and Margaret came, and Margaret asked me who the woman was sitting on the divan. I told her it was someone I had met recently and become friends with—but when I told Margaret her name (her married name) she said, "No it's not! It's Betty Rowland, and I was at school with her."

'So she went and spoke to her—and my friend said, "But Margaret, when you were at school you didn't have a sister. I don't remember you having a sister." And Margaret said, "Well, no, you wouldn't have known about her. She was in hospital." It was a very funny reaction, and it was the sort of thing that had happened all the time. I was either nothing—or I was extra special. But it was not normal, and nobody talked about it. My whole family behaved like that.

'I think that my parents were rather foolish, with the very best intention. They told Rob and Margaret that they must treat me nicely and be kind to me, and more or less suggested that if they didn't I might have a relapse. I'm not sure that my parents actually said that in so many words, but when I did have a relapse and went back into hospital Margaret saw Rob weeping—and he threw a boot at her and smashed her mirror.

'I was always very surprised about that, because I didn't think he was that fond of me. But I was talking to Margaret about it again the other day and she said, "Oh no, it wasn't that, but children always feel guilty if siblings are ill or damaged in some way, and Mother and Dad didn't know that. Irrationally, but understandably, they must have felt guilty too."

'I remember some little things so clearly. One day I gave my father some photographs that I'd had taken on holiday, and I was sitting on the edge of a boat down in Cornwall. He looked at them— then he said, "What a sloppy way you're sitting. Why don't you sit up properly?" I said to him, "Well, it may have escaped your notice, but I can't sit up properly. I have actually been ill and had an operation, and I have got a permanently fixed hip." He just wanted to gloss it all over and pretend it never happened. The best thing was to forget about it. So I couldn't talk about it. No one could.

'When I first came home I could hardly talk English. I spoke French and German, so again there was this extraordinary thing of being very special in a rather peculiar sort of way. And being the object of intense jealousy which nobody dared recognize. I once said something to my brother about my having to achieve so much, and he said, "I don't see why you've got to achieve more than anybody else has"—and a lot of that was the sort of anger and bitterness which they couldn't talk about.'

'Was it because of the attention you were getting and because you were special?' I asked. Barbara nodded. 'That's right.' 'And when did your anger start?' I went on, 'because for the first few years of your life you say you can't remember your feelings. But I know you can be quite angry. So when did that start fizzing?'

Barbara thought for a few moments. 'I don't know that I ever really got angry about all that. I realized how it all messed up my life—education in particular, which I had to battle for, and eventually I got into university. But I think I am an angry person in the sense that I have always felt I have had to battle for everything I got. It was really about survival.'

'People tend to think of me as a very aggressive personality and to get frightened of me. But I think the anger became part of my personality because of my need to survive and to overcome whatever difficulties I had facing me. I wanted to get myself sufficient professional equipment to live my own life and to make myself independent, which I did.

'But I think it cost me the capacity to make really close relation-ships. Because if people became very important to me I would tend to be rather possessive. I would develop a rather intense relation-ship—here is somebody who loves me at last! Then it would break up, and then I wouldn't want to try it again.'

'Are you just talking about relationships with men,' I asked, 'or men and women?' 'I am talking about men and women,' she said. 'But I remember one awful Christmas. My father had been married to my stepmother for three months. My brother had been married ten days. And in another three months Margaret was going to marry Brian. Everybody was calling somebody darling, and all I knew when I heard this was that it wasn't me and I wanted to leave the house. But I had nowhere to go.'

'Do you have a sense of value now, and of worth?' I asked. 'Yes, I have,' she said. So I asked if she knew where it came from.

'I have been trying to write my autobiography—not very successfully,' she told me, 'and it led me into a bit of a depres-sion. But I wanted to call it *Pepsi*. When I went to Switzerland the nurses asked me what my name was and I said "It's Barbara." They said, "But what does your daddy call you?" and I said "Babsy." But they couldn't say Babsy. The Swiss tongue can't get around the Bs. So they said "Pepsi". And the whole of the time I was there I was known as Pepsi—and it occurred to me that this child Pepsi was a secret child that nobody else knew.

'When I came back I brought her with me from this strange place. They had known her there. But nobody else has known her since. So I kept her as my secret child, and I think that she had a value for me. I think that she was me. The core of me, really, and all the secret things I couldn't talk about.

'I certainly helped myself to have a sense of value when by some miracle I got into college. I got into university, and when I was there I had a very painful love affair. So when I came to London I was in a bit of a mess emotionally and I went into therapy. I stayed in therapy for quite a long time, and then I decided to become a psychotherapist. I was a social worker at the time, and all through those years I think that I had a sense of my own value as a social worker and as a psychotherapist. Professionally I was a person of value, who valued other people.'

'Tell me a bit about the God dimension in your life,' I said to her, 'and also about the poetry dimension—because it seems to me that your spirituality expresses itself mostly through poetry.' Barbara nodded.

'Yes. The height of expression of the worship of God seems to me to lie in the poetry of the metaphysicals—George Herbert and John Donne, who also wrote very beautiful erotic poetry. And that said a lot to me, because I didn't know where to put that side of me. I attended the Poetry Society for a long time, and I had always had a sense of what was really good and what was banal. I couldn't stand the idea of worshipping God in anything that was banal—not the God I wanted to worship. The more beautiful something was the more it seemed to me to express the idea of God. I think Ian always understood that.'

Ian was Barbara's local vicar when she had lived in Battersea, and as they had talked over the years she had decided that his sort of Christianity was just what suited her. He had a profound sense of the wonder and the glory of God blended with a deep understanding of humanity and a crisp sense of humour. So she was baptized and received into the Church of England in 1972.

'Will you finish with one of your favourite poems?' I asked, 'but preferably not "Love bade me welcome" because someone else has chosen it.' 'I got someone to read that poem at my baptism,' Barbara said, 'and to read T.S. Eliot—the end of 'Little Gidding'. That's where it all comes together. You have learned everything you have from your life—'and the fire and the rose are one.'

With the drawing of this Love and the voice of this Calling

We shall not cease from exploration
And the end of all our exploring
Will be to arrive where we started
And know the place for the first time.
Through the unknown, remembered gate
When the last of earth left to discover
Is that which was the beginning;
At the source of the longest river
The voice of the hidden waterfall
And the children in the apple-tree
Not known, because not looked for
But heard, half-heard, in the stillness
Between two waves of the sea.
Quick now, here, now, always—
A condition of complete simplicity
(Costing not less than everything)
And all shall be well and
All manner of thing shall be well
When the tongues of flame are in-folded
Into the crowned knot of fire
And the fire and the rose are one.

T.S. Eliot, 'Little Gidding' in *Four Quartets* © 1942 Faber and Faber Limited

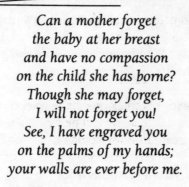

Can a mother forget
the baby at her breast
and have no compassion
on the child she has borne?
Though she may forget,
I will not forget you!
See, I have engraved you
on the palms of my hands;
your walls are ever before me.

Isaiah 49:15–16

People were bringing little childen to Jesus to
have him touch them, but the disciples rebuked
them. When Jesus saw this, he was indignant. He
said to them, 'Let the little children come to me,
and do not hinder them, for the kingdom of God
belongs to such as these. I tell you the truth,
anyone who will not receive the kingdom of God
like a little child will never enter it.' And he took
the children in his arms, put his hands on them
and blessed them.

Mark 10:13–16

7

PRECIOUS CHILD

To ask God to reveal to us how he sees us can be a frightening prospect, as we feel he might show us something horrific that we would rather not face. There are times when we need to see what is inside us in order for God to deal with it and free us from the sin that so easily entangles us.

When we are cleansed and forgiven we are then free to see how much he really loves us—his precious children who need cleaning up and who, instead of squirming in his arms can rest there and know their loving Father's hug.

Precious child

Show me, dear Lord, how You see me through Your eyes,
So that I can realise Your great love for me.
Teach me, O Lord, that I am precious in Your sight;
That as a father loves his child so You love me.

I am Yours because You have chosen me,
I'm Your child because You've called my name.
And Your steadfast love will never change,
I will always be Your precious child.

Show me, dear Lord, that I can never earn Your love;
That a gift cannot be earned, only given.
Teach me, O Lord, that Your love will never fade;
That I can never drive away Your great mercy.

Andy Park © Mercy Publishing/Thankyou Music 1989

Sometimes God has to say to us: 'Listen to me! Listen to what I'm saying to you! I am telling you that I love you. I am telling you that I delight in you. I am telling you that you are precious to me...'

But it sounds too good to be true. We daren't believe it—so we don't listen.

If that is how it is for you, will you read the words of Phil's song 'Precious child' and pray them? Not just once, but over and over again in the coming weeks and months—and if you have the cassette then listen to them as well.

Tracey discovered that love can't be earned by being good—and dieting and getting thin was just one way in which she was trying to be good. She is studying law at Oxford, and plans to get married soon after she has done her finals. She got engaged just a few months ago—and she looks beautifully healthy and very happy.

But a few years ago Tracey wasn't healthy and she wasn't happy. She had an eating disorder and she was getting far too thin.

Tracey's story

'I lost a stone in weight', she said, 'and I could see that it was getting a little bit out of control. But I didn't see it as anything bad. Losing weight was a success. I don't know why I did it. I had a real desire to be good. I always seemed to be striving for something or other and getting thin was another attempt to be good.

'I suppose in worldly terms I was a success. An achiever. I was very good academically and I was OK at games—but I wanted to be good in all the other areas as well.

'I've got a super family and they're very supportive. My parents came from a very poor background and they did very well—so there was a certain pressure on me. Not to be something I couldn't be but to be the best I could be.'

Tracey had a real desire to please her parents, but is aware now that what a parent thinks is the best thing for their child to do isn't necessarily the best thing. 'And it isn't always what you feel is the best,' Tracey said, 'or what you think you're capable of. There was never any pressure on me to do anything impossible—so that I would say, "There's no way in which I could do that." But I knew that I could do some things, and I thought that I had got to strive to do them.'

Since her own difficulty Tracey has talked to a lot of other people who have had problems with eating disorders, and she says that either they didn't feel loved or they didn't get attention at home. 'But I was loved,' she said, 'and I knew that I was. But I don't think any parent can give perfect love, and when you reach your teenage years you start to realize that. I think I equated pleasing my parents with love—with being loved by them.'

As a result of her eating disorder Tracey lost so much weight that she became very anaemic. She was fifteen years old and had problems with her periods. So she went into hospital to have some tests—and also to have a simple exploratory operation.

'When I was in there,' she said, 'I remember thinking that Jesus' love is different—and that what I was doing was silly. It wasn't being good to be getting slim. It was being silly, and what I was doing was quite serious.'

Tracey had never been into hospital before, and she was really scared. 'But when I was being wheeled along to the operating theatre on a trolley I remember thinking in very childlike terms that it was OK, because Jesus loved me. Very childish—but that's what I thought...'

She was thinking in the right way, because Jesus told us that we had to be like a little child: 'I tell you the truth, anyone who will not receive the kingdom of God like a little child will never enter it' (Mark 10:15).

Three months before she went into hospital Tracey had started going back to church. 'I realized there was something wrong in my life,' she said. There was something missing. And I realized how much weight I had lost. I was as thin as you can be without being horribly thin. I wouldn't call myself anorexic—because I did realize that you could be horribly thin. But just getting thin wasn't making any difference. There was just this great gap.'

I wondered how she had filled the gap. 'It was a realization of God's love,' she said. 'It was very gradual and it happened over a year. From that point on things did start to change. There was no dramatic change in terms of eating. But God was changing my attitudes to food in terms of seeing food as good or bad. And over that year I began to realize God's love, and how much God loved me. He communicated his love to me in a few special times.'

'So do you feel a different person now?' I asked. 'Yes,' she said. 'I can say now that I am precious in his sight—and I know when I realized that fully. It was on a Sunday evening at a service in my own church. I had never considered the wrongness of thinking that you are not a valuable person—and I'd never realized that it was a sin. I don't know if it was something in the sermon that got through to me, but at the end of the service I was in tears. I was really crying, and realizing that what I had done was wrong.

'I didn't really understand about forgiveness, and I remember thinking that there would have to be a punishment for what I'd done. I didn't feel angry about it. I thought it was quite right—because of the way I'd treated myself. What came into my mind was that if I got married I would never be allowed to have children. That would be God's punishment for treating my body in the way I had.

'I was just weeping and weeping—and feeling so embarrassed. Then the minister's wife came up, and she started to pray with me. I was too upset to explain anything, but then she read me a few verses from Isaiah 44 about being God's child, and not being afraid because he was with me. Then it goes on to say, "I will bless your offspring." She said to me, "Now God doesn't want you to think that he will never allow you to have children..." Yet I hadn't told her anything about what I was thinking—and at that point I just knew that God loved me and understood me.'

'But now listen, O Jacob, my servant,
Israel, whom I have chosen.
This is what the Lord says—
he who made you, who formed you in the womb,
and who will help you;
Do not be afraid, O Jacob, my servant,
Jeshurun, whom I have chosen.
For I will pour water on the thirsty land,

and streams on the dry ground;
I will pour out my Spirit on your offspring,
and my blessing on your descendants.
They will spring up like grass in a meadow,
like poplar trees by flowing streams.'

Isaiah 44:1–4

I asked Tracey how she lived her Christian life and kept her relationship with God growing. 'I think it's through prayer and Bible study,' she said, 'and being part of a fellowship as well, and having Christian friends. Since I came to my present church I've made Christian friends of my own age, and I've never had any before. The church I went to at home was wonderful, but there just weren't any people of my own age.

'Also I think it helps just to think about things, and to let truths sink into you. A weakness of mine is to be always trying to achieve, and I can see my struggle to live the Christian life as a success and an achievement. So it's important for me just to sit back and realize what God's doing.

'I'm so glad that God sorted things out with me before I got engaged,' she said, 'because it's very easy to look for esteem from other people. And there's a sense in which it's right to receive esteem. But I needed to look to God for it—and I really know now that I am precious in his sight.'

> How great is the love the Father has lavished on us, that we should be called children of God! And that is what we are! The reason the world does not know us is that it did not know him.

1 John 3:1

Love can't ever be earned. It can only ever be given—by a person who is a loving person and whose nature is to love. We love one another imperfectly—even when we are Christians—but God loves us perfectly. God *is* love, and he loves us with an immense love.

Adrian Plass wrote once that 'God is bonkers about us.' He wrote it in *New Daylight*—the Bible Reading Fellowship's daily notes of which I am the editor—and a few people wrote to complain that this was a disrespectful and improper way to write about God. But far more wrote to say how delighted they had been when they read it—and how Adrian's words had got through to them and reached their hearts in a way that more formal language had never done.

One research scientist told a friend that he sometimes stops work for a moment or two and says to himself with great glee: 'God's bonkers about me!'

Glee is 'exultant, high spirited joy' (Webster)—and when the glory of the love of God starts to dawn in our hearts (just a different way of saying that he is bonkers about us) then those are the thoughts and the feelings that start to well up within us.

One of the ways to experience the love of God is to get to know what the Bible says about it. To read, or to listen, and to let the words sink into us. To do that is to listen to God—and the words are living words. Try learning the following passage by heart—and say it quietly to yourself when you are on your own. Or else say it loudly and joyfully.

But God, being rich in faithful love, through the great love with which he loved us, even when we were dead in our sins, brought us to life with Christ—it is through grace that you have been saved—and raised us up with him and gave us a place with him in heaven, in Christ Jesus.

This was to show for all ages to come, through his goodness towards us in Christ Jesus, how extraordinarily rich he is in grace. Because it is by grace that you have been saved, through faith, not by anything of your own, but by a gift from God; not by anything that you have done, so that nobody can claim the credit. We are God's work of art, created in Christ Jesus for the good works which God has already designated to make up our way of life.

Ephesians 2:4–10 (NJB)

Then from time to time reflect on what it means that you are God's work of art. Think about how a great artist pours himself, or herself, into the work of art. A sculptor, or a painter, or a writer... Think of Michelangelo creating David, and spending years painting that incredible ceiling in the Sistine Chapel in Rome. Think of the delight of the artist when the work is finished—and remember the delight of God when he was making the world through wisdom: through Christ, who the New Testament says is the power and the wisdom of God:

'When he marked out the foundations of the earth,
then I was beside him, like a master workman;
and I was daily his delight,
rejoicing before him always,
rejoicing in his inhabited world
and delighting in the sons of men.'

Proverbs 8:29—31 (RSV)

There is a mutual delighting of God the Father and God the Son—and a delighting in us, who are God's work of art. But it isn't only God who does the work. We have to do it with him.

'Therefore, my dear friends,' wrote Paul to the Christians in Philippi, 'as you have always obeyed—not only in my presence, but now how much more in my absence—continue to work out your salvation with fear and trembling, for it is God who works in you to will and to act according to his good purpose' (Philippians 2:12–13).

It isn't that we are to work it out with a feeling of craven fear—but with an awed fear and an awed trembling at the wonder and the glory of it. C.S. Lewis, as always (well, almost always!) gets it right about the glory of the love of God.

When Christianity says that God loves man, it means that God *loves* man: not that He has some 'disinterested', because really indifferent, concern for our welfare, but that, in awful and surprising truth, we are the objects of His love.

You asked for a loving God: you have one. The great spirit you so lightly invoked, the 'lord of terrible aspect', is present: not a senile benevolence that drowsily wishes you to be happy in your own way, not the cold philanthropy of a conscientious magistrate, nor the care of a host who feels responsible for the comfort of his guest, but with the consuming fire Himself, the Love that made the worlds, persistent as the artist's love for his work and despotic as a man's love for a dog, provident and venerable as a father's love for a child, jealous, inexorable, exacting as love between the sexes.

How this should be, I do not know: it passes reason to explain why any creatures, not to say creatures such as we, should have a value so prodigious in their Creator's eyes. It is certainly a burden of glory not only beyond our deserts but also, except in rare moments of grace, beyond our desiring... But the fact seems unquestionable.

C.S. Lewis *The Problem of Pain*, © 1940 HarperCollins, page 35

When I wrote that C.S. Lewis gets it right *almost* always I was quite serious. Because I don't believe that he has got it absolutely right in this beautiful passage. The reason why we have 'a value so prodigious' in the eyes of our Creator is that he created us and that he loves us—and the Old Testament as well as the New tells out that wonderful truth on almost every page. Listen to Isaiah—or, rather, listen to God speaking to you through Isaiah...

But now thus says the Lord,
he who created you, O Jacob,
he who formed you, O Israel:
'Fear not, for I have redeemed you;
I have called you by name, you are mine.
When you pass through the waters I will be with you;
and through the rivers, they shall not overwhelm you;
when you walk through fire you shall not be burned,

and the flame shall not consume you.
For I am the Lord your God,
the Holy One of Israel, your Saviour.
I give Egypt as your ransom,
Ethiopia and Seba in exchange for you.
Because you are precious in my eyes,
and honoured, and I love you,
I give men in return for you,
peoples in exchange for your life.
Fear not, for I am with you;
I will bring your offspring from the east,
and from the west I will gather you;
I will say to the north, Give up,
and to the south, Do not withhold;
bring my sons from afar
and my daughters from the end of the earth,
every one who is called by my name,
whom I created for my glory,
whom I formed and made.'

Isaiah 43:1–7 (RSV)

God cares for the individual, not just for the crowd. The parable that Jesus told about the lost sheep tells us this in such a way that we would be very dull-witted to doubt it.

'Suppose one of you has a hundred sheep and loses one of them. Does he not leave the ninety-nine in the open country and go after the lost sheep until he finds it? And when he finds it, he joyfully puts it on his shoulders and goes home. Then he calls his friends and neighbours together and says, "Rejoice with me; I have found my lost sheep."'

Luke 15:4–6

An old hymn puts that story into poetry—and when I read the words aloud I find myself talking to Christ through them, and hearing him answering the questions that the words ask:

'Lord, thou hast in thy fold thy ninety and nine,
Are they not enough for thee?'
But the shepherd made answer,
'This of mine has wandered away from me.
And although the way be rough and steep
I go to the desert to find my sheep.'
But none of the ransomed ever knew
How deep were the waters crossed.
Or how dark the night that the Lord went through
To rescue his sheep that was lost.

If we don't feel that we are loved and precious in the sight of God then we can pray that we *will* feel it and that we *will* know it. St Paul says in his letter to the Christians in Rome that 'God has poured out his love into our hearts by the Holy Spirit, whom he has given us.' We can't be a Christian at all unless the Holy Spirit lives within us. When we become a Christian—however it happens, and whether we remember the day of our new birth or not—the Holy Spirit enters into our personality.

It is the Holy Spirit within us who makes us really sure that we are the sons and daughters of God, and it is the Holy Spirit who makes us aware of the immense love which God has for us.

For all who are led by the Spirit of God are sons of God. And so we should not be like cringing, fearful slaves, but we should behave like God's very own children, adopted into the bosom of his family, and calling to him, 'Father, Father.' For his Holy Spirit speaks to us deep in our hearts, and tells us that we really are God's children.

Romans 8:14–16 (Living Bible)

It is the Holy Spirit who will also make us aware of our infinite value and preciousness to God—as we pray, and worship, and wait for it to happen. There are some ways to pray about this earlier on in this chapter—and there are some more in the final section of *Value Me*.

It is called *Working with God* because working with God is what we have to do. The living God created us and will be working with us, and delighting in us, and we shall know more and more of his love for us, and our value to him. If we will be still and listen to him—and let him tell us.

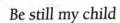

Be still my child

I have loved you
With an everlasting love,
And I have drawn you
With loving kindness,
I will build you up again.

I will hold you
In My everlasting arms;
I will restore you,
With loving kindness.
I will take you to My heart,
I will take you to My heart.

Be still, My child, be still, My loved one
Be still, My child, let Me love you.
Be still, My child, be still, My loved one;
Be still, My child, let Me hold you in My heart.

This is the lullaby of a God who has an eternity of love in store for all his children. The desire of his heart is for the lost to be found, the despairing to be comforted, the broken to be restored, the sick to be healed, the bound to be freed and the poor to be enriched.

'The Lord your God is with you, he is mighty to save. He will take great delight in you, he will quiet you with his love, he will rejoice over you with singing' (Zephaniah 3:17).

Rejoice with Jerusalem, and be glad for her,
all you who love her;
rejoice with her in joy,
all you who mourn over her;
that you may suck and be satisfied
with her consoling breasts;
that you may drink deeply with delight
from the abundance of her glory.

For thus says the Lord:
'Behold, I will extend prosperity to her
like a river,
and the wealth of the nations
like an overflowing stream;
and you shall suck,
you shall be carried upon her hip,
and dandled upon her knees.

As one whom his mother comforts,
so will I comfort you;
you shall be comforted in Jerusalem.
You shall see, and your heart shall rejoice;
your bones shall flourish like the grass;
and it shall be known
that the hand of the Lord is with his servants,
and his indignation is against his enemies.'

Isaiah 66:10–14 (RSV)

WORKING WITH GOD

We have called this section *Working with God* because that is what we shall be doing in it. Paul has told us to 'work out your salvation with fear and trembling, for it is God who works in you to will and to act according to his good purpose' (Philippians 2:12–13).

Our salvation is a gift. But we have to cooperate with God in working it out. We have to put ourselves into the hands of the wounded surgeon to let him work on us and in us. We have to put ourselves into the hands of the diamond cutter and let him change us from dull, rough diamonds into cut diamonds which wonderfully reflect the light of Christ. The presence and the power of Christ is at work within us, but we can resist it and refuse to cooperate. Or we can surrender ourself to the love of God and let him change us 'from glory to glory'. But some of us aren't very aware of our glory. We feel worthless. So let's start there.

A way to pray

Sit on the floor by your bed and cradle your head in your hands. Or sit at a table with your head in your hands. Tell God what you really feel like. Not worth very much. Not a valuable person. Not precious. If you find it painful to admit what you really feel then ask Jesus to help you get in touch with your feelings. Stay there for a little while—from five to fifteen minutes—and then read aloud Isaiah 43:1–4. Then read it aloud again—and instead of the name Jacob, and the name Israel, in the first verse, put in your own name. Spend some more time letting the words sink into you (and perhaps reading them over and over again). And reflect on the fact that it wasn't Egypt that God gave for your ransom—it was himself, in his son. Then either read out the words of the songs, 'I will change your name' and 'Value me' or, if you have the cassette, play them and listen to them.

There is a little child within every one of us who has been hurt, and not loved as much as we needed to be loved. Perhaps for you the lack of loving was because your parents didn't know how to love. Perhaps they had never been loved themselves—or not enough. Perhaps they were wilfully cruel to you. But don't think now about the reasons why it happened. Curl up like a little child by your bed, or by a chair, and ask Jesus to help you. Do what Desmond Tutu does. Become a baby in the presence of God—and ask Jesus to do for you whatever needs to be done. Ask him to comfort you—and remember the promise that he makes in Isaiah: 'As a mother comforts her child, so will I comfort you...' (Isaiah 66:13). Perhaps your mother failed to comfort you and love you as you needed to be comforted and loved. Then read aloud the words that God speaks to you in Isaiah 49:15. 'Can a mother forget the baby at her breast and have no compassion on the child she has borne? Though she may forget, I will not forget you!' Then either listen to 'Comfort to my soul' on the tape or read the words of the song aloud, together with the text which Phil wrote to go with the song.

You can use those ways of praying for all the things in your own life on which you want to work with God. But you will need to use these ways over and over again, because you will have to let the love of God fill the whole of you. That hardly ever happens overnight, and neither does healing. But people sometimes have special experiences of the love of God and of his power to heal—and those things often happen when we are praying with other people and they are praying for us.

Ministering—and receiving ministry

Once you have opened up to God about your feelings of worthlessness—or any other feelings—you will probably need to open up to at least one other person. In *Clinical Theology* Dr Frank Lake wrote that in pastoral ministry three facts invariably accompany one another for good.

> **First, openness towards God in a life of closer obedience, with that alert readiness which arises out of a persistent**

prayer life, so that common talk slips naturally into conversation about the ultimates of existence.

Second, openness towards another [person] about one's own unresolved fears and lusts, rages and depressions, sins and unsuccessful struggles, an openness that may have been hellish hard to reach, over the conventional high walls of religious pride, breached only through prayer and obedience.

Third, an openness towards others, which they can usually recognize before we can. Our own inner openness to God and to another [Christian] brings a new coin into circulation.'

Frank Lake, *Clinical Theology,* © Darton Longman & Todd, 1966

Being open with another person

Find someone you can trust, and tell them about whatever is troubling you. Your low self-esteem. Your lack of value and your sense of worthlessness. Your pain—whatever the cause of it. The way you were abused as a child—in whatever way it was. Tell your story to the person you have chosen, and be as open and as honest as you can. If you find yourself starting to cry as you talk then just let the tears flow. Then let the person pray for you.

Listening to another person

As you listen, use all your attention. Listening takes a great amount of energy, because you are attending at a deep level to another person—and giving them the gift of yourself. You are there and available with all your mind, all your attention and a lot of your strength—for the person who is telling you their heartache and their story. Listening is a form of loving—and as you receive what the person tells you you are also giving yourself to them. As you listen, pray. Not in words—because that would spoil the self-giving of yourself and your attention.

Pray deep inside yourself, without words, but with your heart open to the Holy Spirit, and with a desire and a request for wisdom. The wisdom of God lives within you anyway, because the Spirit of Christ is in you—'Christ the power of God and the wisdom of God'.

When the person who is telling you their troubles and their story has come to an end (at any rate for this time) then pray for them as the Spirit leads you, and read to them from the Bible as the Spirit leads you. Perhaps read out the words of one of Phil's songs, or listen to one of them.

Sometimes it is necessary for a person to seek help from a professionally trained counsellor. If you have been meeting to talk and pray with someone who is suffering from a sense of worthlessness or who has been abused as a child, or who has been emotionally scarred by their experiences, be aware that they may possibly need more help than you are able to give them. Similarly, if you are the person who is suffering, recognize that you may need to get some professional help.

A reflection on a diamond

Imagine a rough diamond buried deep in the earth. No light reaches it there. It looks like a worthless stone. But one day a man finds it, and he knows its value. Just as Jesus knows your value.

Every diamond is unique—made of crystals of carbon. And every crystal is unique. No snowflake is exactly like another snowflake. No diamond is exactly like another diamond. There is no one like you in the whole world. You are unique.

'Even a good quality diamond looks no more than a glassy pebble when it is first pulled out of the ground, and it needs the skilled eye and steady hand of the diamond cutter to release its beauty, turning the rough stone into a dazzling jewel (*Focus on Diamonds*)'.

A diamond may be of good quality or bad quality. The good quality diamonds are worth more than the bad quality ones. But every human being is made in the image and likeness of God—and of infinite value.

'Part of the secret of the beauty of diamonds is their great ability to transmit and reflect light. Even by the light of a single candle, the transparent clarity of a good diamond can make it shine and flash from the other side of a room. As well as brilliance, a diamond has natural "fire"—the name given to its ability to split white light into a dazzling blaze of rainbow colours' (*Focus on Diamonds*).

You have the ability to reflect the light of Christ. 'As you reflect the Lord's glory, you are being transformed into his likeness with ever-increasing glory.' Jesus said, 'I am the light of the world'—and he also said, 'You are the light of the world.'

You can shine with the light of Christ and the glory of God in a way that no one else can in the whole world—because you are unique in the whole world.

'Nearly all diamonds have minor imperfections, called "inclusions", which affect their clarity. These spots, bubbles and lines were formed in the stone when it first crystallized, and are unique to each stone, much like a human finger-print. Perfect flawless diamonds that show no imperfections to a trained eye are very rare' (*Focus on Diamonds*).

Perfect flawless human beings are not just rare. There has only ever been one such in the whole world.

He can take you, with your flaws, and your imperfections, and, as he cuts the diamond that is you to reflect the light that is him, he will take the flaws and the imperfections—all the pain, all the rejection, all the suffering, all the things that have happened to you and all the things you have done—and make you into a human being with a unique glory and a unique shining.

'We know that in all things God works for the good of those who love him...' (Romans 8:28)—and he will take your flaws and imperfections and work them together for good and for glory.

If you have enjoyed reading and using *Value Me*, you may wish to know that BRF produce two regular series of Bible reading notes, *New Daylight* and *Guidelines* which are published three times a year (in January, May and September). *New Daylight* contains printed Bible passages, brief comments and prayers. *Guidelines* contains running commentary on the Bible with a more devotional reflection at the end of each week. *New Daylight* is also available in a large print version.

Copies of *New Daylight* and *Guidelines* may be obtained from your local Christian bookshop or by subscription direct from BRF.

A **FREE SAMPLE COPY** of *New Daylight* or *Guidelines* containing two weeks of readings may be obtained by sending an A5 SAE marked '*New Daylight*' or '*Guidelines*' to BRF.

For more information about *New Daylight*, *Guidelines* and the full range of BRF publications, write to: The Bible Reading Fellowship, Peter's Way, Sandy Lane West, OXFORD OX4 5HG (Tel: 01865 748227)